ABRAHAM
LINCOLN

PRESIDENTIAL ◆ LEADERS

ABRAHAM LINCOLN

JEREMY ROBERTS

LERNER PUBLICATIONS COMPANY / MINNEAPOLIS

Lerner Publications Company
A division of Lerner Publishing Group
241 First Avenue North
Minneapolis, MN 55401 U.S.A

Website address: www.lernerbooks.com

Library of Congress Cataloging-in-Publication Data

Roberts, Jeremy, 1956–
    Abraham Lincoln / by Jeremy Roberts.
      p.   cm. — (Presidential leaders)
    Includes bibliographical references and index.
    Summary: Profiles the self-educated man who arose from poverty to become the sixteenth president of the United States, focusing on how his virtues enabled him to overcome many personal and political difficulties.
      ISBN: 0–8225–0817–6 (lib. bdg. : alk. paper)
      1. Lincoln, Abraham, 1809–1865—Juvenile literature. 2. Presidents—United States—Biography—Juvenile literature. [1. Lincoln, Abraham, 1809–1865. 2. Presidents.] I. Title.
II. Series.
E457.905 .R63 2004
973.7'092—dc21   2002152929

Manufactured in the United States of America
1 2 3 4 5 6 – JR – 09 08 07 06 05 04

CONTENTS

———— ✧ ————

An early photograph of Abraham Lincoln, taken in 1846, shows him before he grew his customary beard. No childhood photos of him are known to exist.

INTRODUCTION

THE WRESTLER

The local kids had heard tell of a newcomer supposed to be so tough he could whip any man in Sangamon County.

Those were fightin' words in the woods of Illinois in 1831. No newcomer got away with a boast like that without proving it—even if it was the man's boss, not him, doing the boasting.

So the Clary's Grove boys, a group of rowdy young men, came down to New Salem and called the stranger out.

"Wrestle?" said one of the gang.

In seconds, a large circle formed around the two men. The local champion was a stocky brute named Jack Armstrong. Folks said he could throw a bull.

Armstrong and the stranger moved together. They danced for a bit. Armstrong pushed in. The stranger, who stood about six four, kept him off with his long arms. He was good, very good, tough, and serious about fighting. The crowd yelled and urged the wrestlers on.

Armstrong started to tire. Finally he resorted to an old trick. He stomped at the stranger's feet, trying to trip him.

This got the newcomer riled. He roared upright, took Armstrong by the throat in his powerful hands, then slapped him down as if he were a rag doll.

The crowd gasped. Armstrong's friends rushed forward to avenge his defeat. But Armstrong jumped up to stop them.

"He's the best feller that ever broke into this settlement," he declared.

The newcomer was no longer a stranger. Soon he would be well known around New Salem and throughout Illinois. He was rough and tough, intelligent though he lacked a formal education. Within ten years, he'd be a lawyer, thanks to his own hard work and studying. A few years after that, he would become one of the state's leading politicians. And eventually, he would be the president of the United States.

His name was Abraham Lincoln.

CHAPTER ONE

ROUGH BEGINNINGS

"He was never in a college or Academy as a student, and never inside of a college or academy building till [or] since he had a law license. What he has had in the way of education, he has picked up."

—Abraham Lincoln, writing about himself in 1860

Abraham Lincoln was born on February 12, 1809, in a one-room cabin on a hardscrabble farm in Kentucky. His father, Thomas, had only recently bought the land and built the cabin. But the ground proved barren and difficult to farm. In 1811 Thomas moved his family—his wife, Nancy Hanks, and their children, Abraham and his older sister, Sarah—to Knob Creek, a more promising spot about thirteen miles away.

At the time, Kentucky was on the western frontier of the young nation. Abraham Lincoln's grandfather had been killed by Indians less than thirty years earlier. Small homesteads,

Thomas Lincoln, Abe's father

——————— ✧ ———————

complete with log cabins, small patches of cleared land, and a cow or two, dotted western Kentucky, Illinois, Indiana, and Ohio. The hard life of a pioneer did not promise riches, but a hard worker could eke out an independent living. While many pioneers prospered, countless others failed due to disease, crop failures, and other hardships.

Children on the frontier were expected to do their share. "Wearing a shirt—no hat or pants—Abe rode a horse hitched to a 'bull-tongue' plow of wood shod with iron," wrote Carl Sandburg, one of Lincoln's most famous biographers. "He helped his father with seed corn, beans, onions, potatoes. He ducked out of the way of the heels of the stallion and brood mares his father kept."

Abe first attended school with his sister Sarah in 1815. The frontier schools were called ABC schools, or blab schools. Students learned lessons by "blabbing" information out loud to memorize it. Abraham learned the alphabet, reading, and arithmetic, but he attended school for only a few weeks or months at a time. Attitudes about education were very different in the early 1800s. Mandatory attendance and truancy laws didn't exist. Many people, including Abraham's parents, could not read or write. Abe later said that his entire schooling "did not amount to one year."

In 1816 the family moved to Indiana, partly because of land disputes and economic problems in Kentucky and partly "on account of slavery," as Abraham later remembered. Thomas Lincoln was opposed to slavery on religious and economic grounds. He wanted to make his home in a state or territory such as Indiana where slavery was outlawed.

Thick woods covered Indiana. During the Lincolns' first winter there, they nearly froze in their small, hastily built cabin. Eight-year-old Abe helped chop down trees and did many other heavy chores. He even shot a wild turkey for food—but only once. Seeing the bird die made him not want to hunt ever again.

───────────────────── ✧ ─────────────────────

This is a reconstruction of the Kentucky log cabin where Abe was born.

Slavery in America

Almost as soon as Europeans arrived in the Americas, they began bringing slaves from Africa. West African kings first began selling captives to Europeans in about 1500. The slaves were usually shipped from Africa to Brazil or the Caribbean region. From there, many were sent to the American colonies.

While many people think of slavery as something that happened only in the southern United States, it was legal throughout North and South America at one time. Quakers (a Christian group devoted to the idea that all people are equal in God's eye) in Pennsylvania were the first Americans to publicly oppose slavery. The constitution of Vermont, adopted in 1777, was the first to ban slavery in the future United States.

When the U.S. Constitution was first adopted in 1788, it upheld the practice of slavery and said that the importing of slaves could not be banned for twenty years (until 1808). Many of the country's founders, even some like George Washington, who owned slaves, hoped that slavery would eventually end.

By the early nineteenth century, most of the North had banned slavery. But in the South, the economy depended on farming. Farming required many laborers, so slavery remained legal. New techniques in farming cotton made slaves even more crucial to agriculture as the nineteenth century went on. Slavery in the South was also defended on social grounds. Many people claimed that blacks were an inferior race meant by God to be treated as beasts.

The issue of slavery strongly divided whites throughout the nation and remained an important political topic through the first half of the 1800s. "Slave states," states where slavery

In 1861 the London Illustrated News *pictured a slave family on the auction block in Virginia. Slave traders sold slaves at auction, and it was not unusual for families to be split up and sold to different slaveholders.*

─────── ✧ ───────

was allowed, and "free states," those where it was not, fought for power. The Missouri Compromise of 1820 attempted to preserve the balance between slave and free states by admitting Missouri to the Union—the United States of America—as a slave state and Maine as a free state. The bill banned slavery in areas north of Missouri's southern boundary. But later acts and decisions would bring the matter to a head.

MILK SICKNESS

By the fall of 1818, the Lincoln family felt at home in Indiana. But as the days began to shorten, a terrible illness struck some local families. Several people came down with a mysterious disease that drained their energy away until they seemed to sink into their beds and die. The pioneers called it "milk sickness." Modern doctors know that it was actually a form of poisoning. Family cows ate a poisonous wild plant, then passed the poison into their milk. Sometime in September, Abraham's mother became sick.

One morning while Abraham was outside, his sister called him to come inside. He didn't want to.

"Abe," she repeated, her voice low and mournful. Reluctantly, he walked into the cabin and stood before the bed where his mother was stretched out. She struggled just to extend her hand.

"Be good and kind," she told her son.

Her tongue brown, her hands cold, Nancy Hanks Lincoln faded away as her eight-year-old son and eleven-year-old daughter called for her.

Thomas Lincoln built a coffin for his wife, as he had for neighbors who had died. She was buried a short walk from the cabin.

HUNGRY FOR BOOKS

One day a little more than a year after Abraham's mother died, his father came home with a stranger. "Here's your new mammy," he told the children as he helped Sarah Bush Johnston Lincoln down from the wagon. Along with some furniture, the new Mrs. Lincoln brought her three children, Sarah Elizabeth, Matilda, and John Johnston, who ranged in age from thirteen to nine. Their father had died a few years earlier.

The expanded Lincoln family got along fairly well. Abraham grew to love his stepmother deeply. Sarah Bush Lincoln encouraged him to "larn [learn] readin', writin' and cipherin' [math]." She often smoothed things over between Abraham and his father, who didn't get along well. One thing that drove them apart was Abe's desire to read as much as he could. To Thomas Lincoln, reading was a waste of time and energy.

But Abe "was hungry for books," remembered Dennis Hanks, a relative who stayed with the Lincolns. Among the books Abraham read were the Bible, *Aesop's Fables, Robinson Crusoe,* and a biography of George Washington.

——————————— ✧
Abe reads by firelight. He was an avid reader and would sometimes walk for miles to borrow a book.

TUSSLES

Young Lincoln also loved to joke around, and he often got into mischief. As he put it in a school notebook:

> *Abraham Lincoln*
> *His hand and his pen,*
> *He will be good,*
> *But God knows when.*

When he was eleven or twelve, Abe began working for others in the area. He split wood, built fences, and slaughtered hogs, earning six dollars a month plus an extra thirty-one cents on butchering days.

———————————— ✧ ————————————

When he wasn't reading, young Abe was often hard at work chopping wood or clearing farmland.

Growing over six feet tall as a teenager, Abraham was as strong as a grown man. And he loved to put that power to work wrestling. Wrestling was a common sport on the frontier.

A few weeks after Abraham's twenty-first birthday in 1830, he helped his family move to a new home in Macon County, Illinois. Once again, Thomas Lincoln was restless and in search of better land. On the way to Illinois, the family dog jumped out of the wagon and fell through the ice in a stream. Few others thought the dog was worth the risk, but Abe jumped into the freezing water, wading up to his waist to pull him out.

ADVENTURE ON THE RIVER

In the winter of 1831, Abraham was yearning for adventure. He soon found a way to fulfill that longing. A shopkeeper named Denton Offutt hired Abe, his cousin John Hanks, and his stepbrother John Johnston to take a boat down the Mississippi River to New Orleans, Louisiana, once the river thawed. Rivers were the main highways at the time. Goods of all sorts were shipped by flatboat (a flat-bottomed boat used to carry freight in shallow water) or by barge to ports where they could be sold. Abe had made a similar trip a few years earlier. Besides the money, the job promised adventure and grand sights.

Offutt told the men to meet him in Springfield, Illinois, when the weather warmed up. Abraham and the others waited restlessly for the winter to end. But when they arrived in Springfield in the spring, neither Offutt nor the boat were anywhere to be seen. The boys found him drunk in a bar. When he sobered up, Offutt told them he still

*Abe found adventure navigating a flatboat
down the Mississippi River.*

---

wanted to hire them, but they'd have to build the barge as well as take it south to New Orleans.

After a month's worth of work building the boat, they were ready to set out. Soon after they did, their boat got hung up on a dam near New Salem, Illinois. The flat-bottomed craft seemed in danger of losing its cargo of bacon, wheat, and corn. But Abe got the boat unstuck by drilling a hole in it and removing enough cargo so the boat floated free. The cargo remained intact. Lincoln's skillful work prompted Offutt to offer him a job running a store when he got back to Illinois.

Abe stayed in New Orleans about a month, seeing the sights. He left no record of his visit. Then, maybe because he'd had enough, maybe because his money ran out, or maybe just because, he returned north to find Offutt and the job he had promised.

CHAPTER TWO

NEW SALEM

*"He studied what he should do—thought of
learning the blacksmith trade—thought of
trying to study law—rather thought he could
not succeed at that without a better education."*

—Abraham Lincoln, writing about himself in 1860

"The preacher—an old line Baptist—was dressed in coarse
linen pantaloons and a shirt of the same material."

Lincoln paused and looked around at the small crowd
hanging onto every word of his tale. He was a newcomer to
New Salem, where he had come to run Offutt's store.
Though still a stranger, Lincoln sensed he could win over
the local crowd with a funny story.

"He rose up in the pulpit and with a loud voice
announced his text thus: 'I am the Christ, whom I represent today.'"

The men snickered as Lincoln mimicked the self-
important preacher.

"About this time," he said, "a little blue lizard ran up underneath his baggy pantaloons."

There were more chuckles as Lincoln described how the minister kept preaching, all the while slapping at the lizard.

"Mr. Lizard had passed the equatorial line of waistband and was calmly exploring that part of the preacher's anatomy which lay underneath the back of his shirt. Things were now growing interesting, but the sermon was still grinding on," said Lincoln. "The next movement on the preacher's part was for the collar button, and with one sweep of his arm off came the . . . linen shirt."

Lincoln's audience laughed at the idea of a minister naked from the waist up in church. Lincoln finished the story: "One old lady in the rear of the room rose up and . . . shouted at the top of her voice, 'If you represent Christ, then I'm done with the Bible.'"

YARN-TELLER, HONEST DEALER

Telling yarns, or tales, was one way of becoming popular in a small community in the days before television, magazines, and computers provided constant entertainment. Another way to gain popularity was by beating the local champion in a wrestling match. Lincoln did both soon after he arrived in New Salem. The new town on the Sangamon River had about one hundred people, and Offutt thought it would be a good place to start his business.

More importantly, Lincoln dealt fairly and honestly with the customers at Offutt's store. As clerk, Lincoln hauled containers of goods back and forth, stocked shelves, and kept the store orderly. He also had to be a good judge of character. In those days, store owners often supplied credit to local customers for months at a time, since cash was scarce for many people.

Lincoln may have been honest, but he wasn't much to look at. His blue pants floated a good inch above his socks. Made by a local seamstress, his homespun clothing was typical of the frontier. Because Lincoln was so tall, however, his clothes fit even worse than most people's.

Though he was in his early twenties, Lincoln hadn't married or even seriously dated. Many more men than women lived on the frontier. Older men who had a steady income from family or business were the most sought-after mates. "Most young men simply had to bide their time until a home, a career, and a wife all came their way," wrote biographer Kenneth J. Winkle.

HOMESPUN CANDIDATE

On March 9, 1832, an article appeared in the local newspaper that began, "Fellow Citizens: Having become a candidate for the honorable office of one of your representatives in the next General Assembly of this state . . . it becomes my duty to make known to you . . . my sentiments with regard to local affairs."

The article was signed by Abraham Lincoln, who at only twenty-three years old had been persuaded to run for election to the Illinois state legislature. Well liked, Lincoln was seen by townspeople as an intelligent young man who would help the area. Lincoln never said why he decided to enter politics. He did, however, spend much of his time talking about public affairs while running the store. He wasn't intimidated by crowds, and he felt he could bring improvements to New Salem.

Lincoln's campaign statement mostly concerned improvements to the Sangamon River—to make it more navigable by deepening it and controlling its flow—so it could be used to transport goods. This was a popular idea in New Salem, which would benefit from increased trade. Lincoln also mentioned that he thought "every man" should be educated.

"Every man is said to have his peculiar ambition," Lincoln wrote. "I can say for one that I have no other so great as that of being truly esteemed by my fellow men, by rendering myself worthy of their esteem. How far I shall succeed . . . is yet to be developed."

MILITIA CAPTAIN

Before the election for the state assembly was held, Lincoln stood for another post—captain of the local militia, the volunteer army formed to defend the state. That spring about two thousand Sauk and Fox Indians, led by Chief Black Hawk, attempted to return to their native land in Illinois from territory in Iowa. The governor of Illinois called for local volunteers to help federal

————————— ✧
Chief Black Hawk
tried to keep white settlers
from taking lands originally
belonging to the Sauk people.

troops turn the Indians back. Lincoln joined the state volunteer army for several reasons. One was the simple fact
that he needed money. Offutt's store was going bust, and
Lincoln knew he'd soon be out of work. He probably also
realized that military service would help his candidacy. And
like many young men, he may have felt that the war would
be an adventure.

Local militias selected company captains by vote. Lincoln won easily. His main qualification was popularity—
he'd had no military training. He was, however, big and
strong. That counted for something, as did his bravery and
his strong sense of right and wrong. At one point, he stood
between some of his men and an old Indian they wanted to
hang as a spy. Lincoln prevented the man's murder.

Lincoln served for a month as captain, then reenlisted
twice more, serving as a private. He never saw any real
fighting. "I had a good many bloody struggles with the
mosquitoes," he joked later. "Although I never fainted from
loss of blood, I can truly say I was often very hungry."

A NEW STORE

If Lincoln had thought military service would help him win
the election, he was wrong. He lost. But he did discover
another important interest during the war—the law. While
in the militia, he met John T. Stuart, a Springfield lawyer
who was serving as a major. Lincoln borrowed law books
from Stuart and others to learn the profession.

Lincoln received $125 for serving with the army. He
used much of the money to start a new general store with
another New Salem resident, William Berry. Berry proved
to be a bad businessman, drinking much of the store's

liquor. The two young men were soon heavily in debt, and their store failed. Unlike Offutt and many others who simply ran off when their business went broke, Lincoln decided that he would pay off the store's debts. It's not clear how much money he owed, though it probably ranged between $500 and $1,100. The amount increased when Berry died without paying off his share. It took Lincoln at least five and maybe as many as fifteen years to pay the money back. But his slow, steady payments became an important cornerstone of his reputation. His integrity was increasingly evident to others.

Lincoln learned surveying (measuring property lines so that land ownership can be recorded) and took a variety of jobs. In 1833 he was appointed postmaster, a part-time position. Mail came to New Salem only about once a week. Besides the pay, Lincoln could read all the newspapers that came in and had a chance to get to know everyone in the area. That put him in a much better position to run for office in 1834.

A WHIG

In the early 1830s, there were two major political parties in the United States: the Democrats, formed during Thomas Jefferson's time, and the Whigs. The Whig Party had grown out of various other parties in the early 1800s, mostly to oppose the Democrats. Unlike the Democrats, the Whigs proposed a tariff, or tax, on foreign goods that would make American goods cheaper than products imported from foreign countries. The Whig Party appealed to many people like Lincoln who wanted the country to develop its own industries and improve internal commerce, or business.

Even though he was a Whig, however, Lincoln won Democratic backing in his race for the state legislature.

Lincoln's campaign speeches were brief and filled with jokes. A typical one went something like this:

> My politics are short and sweet, like the old woman's dance. I am in favor of a national bank. I am in favor of . . . a high protection tariff. These are my sentiments and political principles. If elected, I shall be thankful; if not, it will all be the same.

Whether it was his short speeches or the fact that many voters knew him personally, Lincoln won the seat easily with 67 percent of the vote.

LOVE LOST

Lincoln's interests were not all politics, business, and the law. Sometime in 1835, after joining the state legislature, he began seeing a young woman named Ann Rutledge. Ann was the daughter of a New Salem tavern owner. She managed the four-room inn above the tavern. Lincoln asked her to marry him.

Not many details of their courtship and engagement are known. Some historians and biographers have questioned whether the two were really engaged. But most scholars believe that the couple had reached an understanding sometime before the summer.

That August Ann fell sick. The disease she had was known locally as "brain fever." Modern doctors believe it was probably typhoid, possibly caused by water from a contaminated well. Only a few days after Ann took to her bed, she went into a coma and died.

After Ann's death, one of her brothers wrote that Lincoln "plunged in despair, and many of his friends feared that reason would desert her throne." William H. Herndon, who became Lincoln's law partner and later wrote a biography of him, believed that Ann's death affected Lincoln for the rest of his life and contributed to severe mood swings and depression. Most other historians, however, believe that mild depression or "hypochondria," as it was called then, was part of his personality even before Ann's death.

Lincoln was back at work soon after Ann's death. A year or so later, he began seeing another woman, Mary Owens. Unsure whether he loved her or not, he broke off the relationship—then offered to marry her! She declined.

Although Lincoln's love life had stalled, his career was moving forward. His law studies had paid off. In the fall of 1836, he was admitted to the Illinois bar, which meant that he could practice law in that state. John Stuart invited Lincoln to join as junior partner in his firm, and Lincoln jumped at the chance. He moved to Springfield in the spring of 1837.

——————— ✧
Lincoln's law partner John Stuart later served in the U.S. Congress.

CHAPTER THREE

SPRINGFIELD

"If what I feel were equally distributed to the whole human family, there would not be one cheerful face on the earth."

—Abraham Lincoln, writing in January 1841, after his breakup with Mary Todd

Carrying his saddlebags, Abraham Lincoln approached the young Springfield storekeeper. Lincoln tossed the bags on the counter and asked the man, Joshua Speed, about the cost for furniture and the fixings for a new bed.

Speed picked up his slate and chalked up the sum: seventeen dollars.

"It is probably cheap enough," said Lincoln, who was only a few years older than Speed. "But I want to say that, cheap as it is, I have not the money to pay. But if you will credit me until Christmas, and my experiment here as a lawyer is a success, I will pay you then. If I fail in that, I will probably never pay you at all."

Joshua Speed became one of Lincoln's closest friends.

——————— ✦ ———————

Speed looked up into the tall stranger's face. It was sincere and so gloomy that Speed almost cried.

"I think I can suggest a plan by which you will be able to attain your end without incurring any debt," Speed told him. "I have a very large room and a very large double bed in it, which you are perfectly welcome to share with me if you choose."

"Where is your room?"

"Upstairs."

Lincoln hoisted his saddlebags over his shoulder and went upstairs. A minute later, he returned without the bags.

"Well Speed, I'm moved," he said. Lincoln had just made one of his best friends for life.

Along with other young men, he and Speed spent many nights over the next few years sitting around the fireplace in the store, swapping yarns and discussing the law, politics, and whatever else happened to interest them.

LAWYER AND LEGISLATOR

Springfield in 1837 had fewer than two thousand people. But for central Illinois, it was a big city and one that was transforming itself. The city was experiencing a building boom. And it had just become the state capital—thanks largely to Lincoln, who had organized legislative support to move the capital from New Salem.

Stuart, a prominent Whig, had decided to run for Congress. That was one reason he'd asked Lincoln to join him in his law firm. Though still a new lawyer, Lincoln handled a wide variety of cases. Fees were usually about five dollars—not a great sum even then but enough for a good living if the firm remained busy. The money Lincoln earned from "lawyering" was supplemented by his pay as a part-time state legislator. He was already a fairly impor-tant member of the legislature, though the votes during the session didn't always go his way.

SLAVE VOTE

In Illinois, as in the rest of the country, slavery was a con-troversial issue. Abolitionists, or people who wanted to abolish slavery, waged a moral and religious cam-paign against it. The aboli-tionists ranged from the fiery William Lloyd Garri-son to the calm and more moderate James Russell Lowell. People everywhere debated laws that supported slavery directly or indirectly, such as those requiring that

————————————— ✧
Abolitionist William Lloyd Garrison published the radical and influential antislavery journal The Liberator.

escaped slaves be returned to their owners, no matter where the slaves were.

Like the other northern states, Illinois banned slavery. However, it bordered two slave states, and many Illinois residents had lived in places where slavery was allowed. In 1837 the Illinois General Assembly passed a resolution condemning abolitionists and proclaiming slavery a sacred right. Lincoln and another legislator wrote a protest declaring that slavery was unjust and hurt the nation. They also said that the emotional arguments and sometimes violent actions of the abolitionists didn't help erase the evil of slavery. Lincoln believed that logic and the law were superior to violence and emotion. But in 1837, these views were in the minority. The legislature adopted the bill over his protests.

MARY TODD

The important young people in Springfield often found themselves at the home of Ninian and Elizabeth Edwards, a prominent couple who owned a mansion in town. Their parties featured dancing, gossip, and plenty of fun. At one of these parties in 1839, an energetic and attractive young woman took Lincoln's arm in a dance.

She was Elizabeth's sister, Mary Todd. Born in 1818, she had a pretty, round face with blue-gray eyes and dark brown hair. Mary was the daughter of a banker and merchant in Lexington, Kentucky. In many ways, she and Abraham were opposites. Lincoln was tall and thin, while Mary was short and plump. He was self-taught and coldly logical. She was well educated and emotional. Her family was well-off, and his was poor. She liked nice clothes and refined social gatherings. Lincoln was rough in almost every

Mary Todd, shown at age 28, was known for her quick temper.

─────── ✧ ───────

way. But the opposites attracted. Abraham told Mary that he wanted to dance with her "in the worst way" when he first saw her at the party. She laughed, but he did get the dance. Soon he was in love.

Mary had another suitor: Stephen Douglas, a young, prominent Democrat. Douglas had a bright future and in many ways was more polished than Lincoln. But by the fall of 1840, Lincoln had clearly won Mary's heart. They talked about getting married and may even have set a date for the wedding.

Then Lincoln got cold feet. He went to tell Mary he didn't love her and to break off the engagement. But when he began talking, Mary became upset. She was so distressed that he changed his mind about breaking it off. But she had gotten enough of a hint, and soon afterward she sent him a letter ending the engagement. Instead of being relieved, Lincoln was very depressed. His friend Speed took the razor from Lincoln's room, worried that he would attempt suicide.

Historians have long debated why Lincoln broke off the engagement. Some said that he might have thought he couldn't supply Mary with the luxuries she wanted. Others have seen a pattern in his romantic relationships and think that Lincoln was simply afraid of commitment.

Whatever Lincoln's reason for getting cold feet, he seemed to realize soon afterward that he had made a mistake. After recovering from his depression, he started to see Mary again. Their love rekindled. Lincoln saw that his friend Speed got married and seemed happy. This encouraged

✧ —————————

Abraham and Mary's marriage certificate

Lincoln, and once more he asked Mary Todd to marry him. She agreed, and the two were married on November 4, 1842.

Even then Lincoln may not have been 100 percent in favor of marriage. Just before the ceremony, a friend remarked that Lincoln looked as if he were a bull about to be slaughtered.

LINCOLN'S DUEL

In September 1842, Abraham Lincoln got off the ferry at Alton, Missouri, with three friends. Lincoln had crossed the river from Illinois to engage in a sword fight.

It sounded like a joke and may have started as one, but the swords and the duel were very real. Some weeks before, Lincoln had written a political letter making fun of a prominent Democrat named James Shields. He got some help from Mary Todd Lincoln, who wrote a similar letter with a friend. Although the letters were anonymous, Shields quickly discovered that Lincoln was one of the authors, and Lincoln took credit for the other letter to protect the ladies.

The two men traded insults, and Shields challenged Lincoln to a duel. Lincoln accepted, suggesting swords as weapons. He may have thought that his longer reach would give him the edge in a fight. Since duels were illegal in Illinois, the two men set an appointment to meet across the river to settle their differences.

At the last minute, however, a mutual friend suggested a face-saving compromise involving a clarification that amounted to an apology. The sword fight was averted.

Though he often made light of himself, Lincoln rarely mentioned the duel and never joked about it. It seems to have been one of the few things in his life he was ashamed of.

Lincoln shared a law office in downtown Springfield.

CHAPTER FOUR

CONGRESSMAN LINCOLN

*"I am not an accomplished lawyer. I find
quite as much material for a lecture in those
points wherein I have failed, as in those
wherein I have been moderately successful."*
—Abraham Lincoln, *Notes on the Practice of Law*

Abraham Lincoln's long face furled into a frown as the man
described his case. Every so often, Lincoln would stop him
with a question, then go back to listening. It was a common
sight in the third-floor office of Logan and Lincoln. The
partners, along with their young student, William "Billy"
Herndon, were one flight up from the state courtroom in
the new Tinsley Building in downtown Springfield.

The man's story finally finished, Lincoln hesitated. He
told the man to come back in an hour. Lincoln spent the
time thinking over the facts he had heard. "You are in the
wrong," he told the man flatly later. Most lawyers would
have avoided saying anything like this, since it could cost

them the client's business. "I advise you to compromise," Lincoln concluded.

AN HONEST LAWYER

Lincoln's reputation as an honest lawyer built up gradually from hundreds of such encounters. He could be counted on to analyze a case objectively, giving his opinion without thinking about his fee. In the courtroom, his clear and concise arguments, spiced with humor, often won the case.

Lincoln left the state legislature at the end of 1842. He planned to run for U.S. Congress in 1843. He had to compete with several other Whigs for the nomination. One of his opponents was his own law partner, Stephen Logan, with whom he had partnered after Stuart's election to Congress. But the real battle proved to be with candidates Edward D. Baker and John Hardin. Fortunately, the fight had a peaceful ending. They decided to rotate the nomination among the three of them over the next few terms.

Hardin won the first designation and then the election in 1843. He made way for Baker in 1844. According to the plan, Lincoln would run in 1846. Meanwhile, Lincoln continued to practice law in Springfield and around the Eighth Circuit in Illinois, an area of about eleven thousand square miles.

Twice a year, the judge responsible for the circuit traveled to the little towns and settlements in the area to hear cases. Most had to do with debts and minor disputes. A small group of lawyers, including Lincoln, traveled with the judge to help local attorneys present their cases. Each trip lasted at least ten weeks. The lawyers shared cramped quarters at local inns, sometimes sleeping two or three to a bed.

Lincoln and his wife spent their honeymoon at the Globe Tavern—and never left. The couple lived there for the first two years of their marriage.

A GROWING FAMILY

Meanwhile, Mary Todd Lincoln was pregnant with the couple's first child. Robert Todd, named after Mary's father, was born August 1, 1843.

Since their marriage, the Lincolns had lived in the Globe Tavern, a small inn near the center of town. The fall after Robert Todd was born, they rented a three-room house. In 1844 they bought a small home at the corner of Eighth and Jackson Streets, paying twelve hundred dollars in cash and trading a piece of property worth about three hundred dollars.

While Lincoln was away on business trips, Mary kept busy. Besides cooking and cleaning, she had to make fires for heating and cooking, pump water from a well, and sew her own clothes. As the Lincolns grew more prosperous, she could afford to hire maids, but Mary's temper and high standards made it difficult for her to keep help. At the same time, she was often anxious and highly emotional. She was afraid of many things, from robbers to dogs, and her fears often got the best of her. Thunder could throw her into a panic. She quarreled with neighbors and maids, as well as her husband. Her disputes with Lincoln sometimes turned vicious. Once, when the fire in the house was going out, she asked him to tend to it. For some reason, he forgot. She asked again. He forgot again. When Mary entered the room for the third time and saw that the fire had gone out, she took a stick and hit Lincoln in the nose.

Historians have taken different views of Mary's mental health as well as her relationship with Lincoln. David Herbert Donald, for example, believes that Mary's well-known outbursts were due to overwork and exhaustion. Others, however, believe she suffered from psychological disorders. Jean H. Baker, who wrote an important biography of Mary Todd Lincoln, declared that she suffered from narcissism, a personality disorder marked by an exaggerated sense of self-importance. Another writer used Mary as a case study of a personality disorder called borderline personality. Sufferers usually exhibit violent mood swings and emotional outbursts. In the 1840s, however, the field of psychology did not exist. If Mary did have a mental illness, it could not be diagnosed or treated. In addition to her possible psychological problems, Mary suffered extreme headaches and severe menstrual cramps.

Lincoln tolerated Mary's outbursts, often treating them like necessary rainstorms. He seems to have loved his wife deeply despite them. For her part, Mary continually encouraged her husband's political ambitions and did whatever she could to support him. She defended her husband fiercely whenever anyone insulted him or compared him unfavorably to his political rivals.

NO "OPEN SCOFFER"
The Lincolns' second child was born in March 1846. He was named Edward Baker, after the Whig congressman.

ABRAHAM LINCOLN, POET

Abraham Lincoln is remembered for many achievements, but writing poetry isn't one of them. Even so, he did try his hand at the art. In 1846 he penned a poem about returning to his old home in Illinois.

> My childhood's home I see again,
>   And sadden with the view;
> And still, as memory crowds my brain,
>   There's pleasure in it too.

The poem continues for several stanzas as Lincoln shows how much things change and fade into the past:

> Where many were, but few remain
>   Of old familiar things;
> But seeing them, to mind again
>   The lost and absent things.

A few months later, the congressman stepped aside to let Lincoln run for office. Opposing Lincoln in the election was Peter Cartwright, a Methodist preacher. As the election neared, Cartwright and his supporters charged that Lincoln was "an open scoffer at Christianity"—someone who didn't believe in God. In response, Lincoln wrote a handbill, or pamphlet, summing up his feelings on religion.

"I am not a member of any Christian church," he noted, "but I have never spoken with intentional disrespect of religion in general, or of any denomination of Christians in particular." Lincoln went on to say that he had earlier believed in a kind of fate that made people act a certain way, but he had abandoned that idea. He also said he couldn't support anyone for office who was an "open enemy of, and scoffer at, religion."

Lincoln did not say directly what he believed. He seems to have believed in God but didn't feel the need to belong to a church. He had read the Bible and knew its stories well. And he had a deep sense of morality. As he grew older, Lincoln's speeches frequently included references to "the Almighty."

Lincoln went on to win the congressional election easily. He, Mary, and the boys moved to Washington, D.C., in the fall of 1847.

CONGRESSMAN LINCOLN

The Lincolns lived near the Capitol in a boardinghouse, where they shared a single room. The boys played noisily inside while their father went off to work. His lanky frame made him stand out in the crowd, but he was not well known when he first arrived in Congress.

Lincoln's name appeared on the Whig Party ticket in 1846.

————————————— ✧

WHIG TICKET.

For Congress.
Abraham Lincoln.

For Governor,
T. M. Killpatrick.

For Lieut. Governor.
N. G. Wilcox.

For Representative.
Stephen T. Logan,
Benjamin West,
James N. Brown,
Rezin H. Constant.

For Sheriff.
William Harvey

For County Commissioner.
Thomas Shepherd.

For Coroner,
James W. Neal.

For a Convention.

Lincoln aimed to change that. Soon after the congressional session began, he led an attack on President James Polk and the Mexican War. The war had begun in 1846, following a series of disputes over Mexican debts to the United States and the U.S. takeover of Texas.

A dispute about the Texas border escalated into fighting. But other factors contributed. A civil war in Mexico had brought leaders to power who were anti-American. Their statements and actions helped inflame American public opinion against Mexico. And President Polk and his advisers saw the war as a way to claim California for the United States.

U.S. forces won easy victories over the disorganized Mexican army in 1846 and early 1847, before Lincoln had even left for Washington. The army occupied Mexico City in September.

During his campaign, Lincoln had supported the men enlisting in the war, even though he may have had some doubts about the war. Once he got to Congress, he became convinced that Polk had lied about how the war started and had acted unconstitutionally. Lincoln and other Whigs also feared that the territory won in the war would be made into slave states.

Lincoln attacked the conflict with Mexico as immoral. His speech in Congress marked him as a leader of the Whigs. But it also cost him support back home, where the war was popular. Most people there and throughout the country backed expansion and looked down on the Mexicans. They did not care about the constitutional issues or whether Polk had lied. (Historians generally agree with Lincoln's interpretation.)

Although the Whigs opposed the war, they used it for political gain. In the 1848 presidential election, the party nominated Zachary Taylor, the general who had led American forces to victory. Lincoln was one of the Whig Party members who

✧ —————————

Mexican War hero Zachary Taylor served as the twelfth president of the United States, from 1849 to 1850. Abraham Lincoln helped Taylor win the election.

helped get Taylor the nomination. That September Lincoln traveled throughout New England campaigning for Taylor, then returned to Illinois to campaign there. Taylor won the election, beating Democrat Lewis Cass and former president Martin Van Buren, who ran as an antislavery Democrat in what was called the Free Soil Party. The three-way race reflected the political divisions that fractured the country.

VOTING AGAINST SLAVERY

Much of the debate in Congress after the presidential election focused on whether slavery should be allowed in the new territories that would be carved from the land given up by Mexico. Lincoln voted for the Wilmot Proviso to ban slavery in these areas, but this provision never became law.

The harsh realities of slavery and racism were on display in the nation's capital. Slavery was legal in Washington, D.C., as it was throughout most of the South. Still, it was a highly charged issue. Many citizens opposed it morally and economically. Others defended it for the same reasons. Those who wanted slavery abolished disagreed about how to do so. Some supporters did not want slavery to be allowed in new territories.

Lincoln opposed slavery, but he did not believe that it could be eliminated immediately. He wanted to limit it to the states where it already existed. He thought his approach would cause slavery to eventually die out.

In early 1849, Lincoln worked on a law that called for a public vote to end slavery in Washington, D.C. If passed, the law would free all slaves except personal servants of federal officers. It also would pay their owners. The law was seen as a compromise between the extremes of allowing slavery or immediately abolishing it without compensation. But his measure lost support once it became public. Both pro-slavery and antislavery groups attacked it.

"Finding that I was abandoned," said Lincoln, "I dropped the matter knowing that it was useless to prosecute [continue] the business."

BACK HOME

Lincoln had said he would serve only one term as congressman, so he did not run for reelection. He was an important member of the Whig Party, and he hoped to get a job as commissioner of the General Land Office, a key political post. But President Taylor gave the job to someone else. He offered to make Lincoln governor of the Oregon Territory instead.

"When he brought the proposition home to fireside," Herndon later claimed, "his wife put her foot squarely down on it with a firm and emphatic no. That always ended it with Lincoln."

Lincoln also may have turned down the job because he saw it as a political dead end. Back in Springfield, the forty-year-old went back to work as a lawyer. Since 1844 he had been partnering with Herndon, now a full-fledged lawyer. Their cases ranged from matters tried in local courts to U.S. Supreme Court cases. By this time, Lincoln was known to other lawyers as Old Honest Abe. His clients included large railroad companies, which increased both his prestige and his income.

A Partner's Biography

Shortly after Lincoln's death, his law partner, William (Billy) Herndon, began gathering notes on Lincoln's life. In 1866 he and his collaborator, Jesse W. Weik, set out to write a biography. The manuscript, *Herndon's Lincoln: The True Story of a Great Life*, was eventually published in 1889. It remains available in different editions in many public libraries.

Herndon and Weik drew on many sources for the book. One of the most important was Herndon himself, who had worked with Lincoln. But the authors also spoke to others who had known Lincoln. They gathered a large collection of letters and notes from interviews with people who had known Lincoln. To this day, the biography and the notes and letters are among the most important secondary sources of information on Lincoln's life. (Lincoln's own writings and other records from the time are considered primary sources.)

Historians have debated many of the claims in Herndon's book. For example, Herndon blames Lincoln's lifelong bouts of depression on the unhappy ending of his love affair with Ann Rutledge. Not only do many historians question this idea, but several concluded that Herndon was mistaken in reporting—and perhaps even invented or exaggerated—the entire affair. Scholars have also argued that Herndon was too close to Lincoln to be objective.

More recently, however, many of those studying Herndon's work have concluded that, while he and his sources may have gotten things wrong, on the whole his work remains important and largely correct.

The different opinions about Herndon serve as a reminder that history is a living thing, often open to interpretation. Opinions and even "facts" can change over time.

A CHANGED FUTURE

In 1850 the Lincolns' youngest son, Edward, died after a two-month bout with tuberculosis. Mary had recently lost her father and grandmother, and Lincoln's father, to whom he was not close, was also ill and dying. Both Lincoln and Mary suffered greatly. At the end of the year, however, Mary gave birth to a third son, William (Willie) Wallace Lincoln, and in 1853, a fourth, Thomas (usually called Tad), was born. Willie soon became Lincoln's favorite. He liked to bring him and Tad into the law office, where their playful antics pestered Herndon. Lincoln was an indulgent, loving father to his two youngest sons, often caring for them at a time when it was considered unusual for a man to take care of children.

Under other circumstances, Lincoln might have remained in the background of party politics for the rest of his life. He could have continued to practice law, enjoying his boys and his local status. But in 1854, the issue that had been simmering for many years in the United States exploded in a way that changed American history forever. In that year, Congress and the president opened all U.S. territories to slavery by reversing the Missouri Compromise of 1820.

Lincoln was outraged by the act *and* by its main supporter— Stephen Douglas, the Illinois senator who had once wanted to marry Mary Todd.

——————————— ✧

William Herndon, one of Lincoln's law partners and biographers

CHAPTER FIVE

SPEECHES AND DEBATES

*"I am not a Know-Nothing. That is certain.
How could I be? How can anyone who abhors
the oppression of negroes be in favor of degrading
classes of white people? Our progress in
degeneracy appears to me to be pretty rapid. . . . "*
—Abraham Lincoln, writing to his friend
Joshua Speed

"My first impulse would be to free all the slaves, and send them to Liberia," said Lincoln. His words stunned many in the large audience in Peoria, Illinois, who had gathered to hear him debate Senator Douglas. "But a moment's reflection would convince me that whatever high hope (as I think there is) there may be in this in the long run, its sudden execution is impossible. If they were all landed there in a day, they would all perish in the next ten."

The crowd rustled nervously. The two men were debating the Kansas-Nebraska Act of 1854, which had become

Stephen Douglas, nicknamed the Little Giant, debated Lincoln many times on the issue of slavery.

✧ ——————————

law several months earlier. The act created two new territories, Kansas and Nebraska, and allowed for voters in each territory to decide whether slavery would be legal when their territory became a state. The act also ended the Missouri Compromise, which had preserved the balance between slave and free states. This meant that both territories could become slave states if they chose. Rather than declining, slavery was advancing.

Lincoln and Douglas weren't just arguing about slavery. They were also trying to get members of their political parties elected to the state legislature.

Many of the people in the Peoria audience were Douglas supporters. They had stood in the sun for three hours that afternoon, October 16, 1854, as Douglas defended his bill. Even most citizens who hated slavery were against legal equality for black people and didn't want them living in their community. Lincoln, as he often did in the courtroom, directly addressed his audience's fears and prejudices, some of which he may have shared. He dismissed the idea—popular at the time—of sending the slaves to Liberia, a territory in western Africa, and then moved on.

As usual when he started a speech, his voice was squeaky and high pitched. But it smoothed out, and he soon spoke in strong, confident tones. He assured the audience that he shared the common prejudice about blacks: they were not "politically and socially our equals." But, he said, all men, regardless of their color, had the rights cited in the Declaration of Independence and the Constitution.

Partly because of Lincoln's efforts, but also because of opposition to the Kansas-Nebraska Act and other factors, the Democrats did poorly in elections that November. One

Despite Lincoln's ungainly appearance and physical awkwardness, his powerful words could fire up a crowd.

Whig who didn't even want the job—Lincoln—won election to the Illinois assembly.

Lincoln had been nominated "in the face of his unwillingness and over his protests," remembered Herndon. Lincoln didn't want to be in the Illinois General Assembly, because he had his eye on the U.S. Senate, where he could directly oppose Douglas. After Lincoln was elected to the state legislature, he resigned to run for the Senate.

At the time, U.S. senators were chosen by state governments. While the state legislators could vote for anyone, they usually selected a member of their own party. The more members of his own party a candidate had in the state legislature, the better his chances of election to national office were.

The state legislators met to elect a senator on February 8, 1855. On the first ballot, Lincoln pulled forty-five votes, six short of a majority. James Shields, a pro-slavery Democrat who closely sided with Douglas, finished second with forty-one. Since neither man had an overall majority, the vote was held again. And again. And again.

Lincoln's votes slowly drained away. A new Democratic choice emerged—Governor Joel A. Matteson, another pro-slaver. Fearing the popular governor would win, Lincoln threw his support to Lyman Trumbull, a Democrat who opposed Douglas and slavery. Thanks to Lincoln, Trumbull won.

"I regret my defeat moderately," Lincoln told a friend. He was happy, he said, that he had at least cut off the pro-slavery candidate.

THE CASE AGAINST SLAVERY

The next few years were busy in Lincoln's law practice. In one famous case, Lincoln proved the innocence of a man accused of murder by showing that the moon was not out when a witness claimed it was.

But politics remained Lincoln's main concern. He continued to struggle with the issue of slavery. Trying to pull together his ideas in some personal notes, he wrote:

> *If A. can prove, however conclusively, that he may, of right, enslave B.—why may not B. snatch the same argument, and prove equally, that he may enslave A?—*
>
> *You say A. is white, and B. is black. It is color then; the lighter having the right to enslave the darker? Take care. By this rule, you are to be slave to the first man you meet with a fairer skin than your own.*
>
> *You do not mean color exactly? You mean the whites are intellectually the superiors of the blacks, and therefore have the right to enslave them? Take care again. By this rule, you are to be slave to the first man you meet with an intellect superior to your own.*

A REPUBLICAN

The slavery issue helped break apart the Whig Party. Many antislavery Whigs were leaving to join a new political party that would be known as the Republican Party. Others joined a party opposed to immigration, the Native American Party, which had started in New York in 1843. Members were known as nativists or Know-Nothings because they often held secret meetings and refused to share any information with the public.

The collapse of the Whigs left Lincoln without a party. If he wanted to run for office again, he'd have to find a new one. Lincoln had opposed Democrats all his political life. And he couldn't join the Know-Nothings, because they vowed to elect only native-born Americans. Lincoln dismissed this as unfair, an unequal treatment of people under the Constitution.

His opposition to slavery drew him to the Republican Party. For a time, though, he chose not to publicly link himself with the Republicans. Herndon forced the issue while Lincoln was away by signing Lincoln's name to a Republican meeting notice that was then published. Lincoln, uncomfortable with the abolitionists who were associated with the Republicans, telegrammed Herndon, "All right; go ahead. Will meet you—radicals and all."

The Illinois Republican Party officially formed at Bloomington, Illinois, on May 29, 1856. Lincoln gave a speech against slavery "amid deafening applause," as Herndon described it. He later received 110 votes for the vice presidential nomination, but another Republican won. The party's presidential candidate, John C. Frémont, a California senator who had won fame as an explorer in the West, ran against Democrat James Buchanan and lost.

Many Americans were wrestling with the subject of slavery. Among them were the justices of the U.S. Supreme Court. In 1857 they issued the Dred Scott decision, inflaming passions on both sides of the issue. Dred Scott, a slave from Missouri, had lived with his owner in Illinois and the Wisconsin Territory before returning to Missouri. In 1846 Scott sued for his freedom. He claimed that because slavery was forbidden in the Wisconsin Territory, he had become a

Dred Scott's fight for his freedom set the stage for a nationwide battle over slavery.
———————— ✧

free man. The case had taken nearly a decade to reach the highest court in the land.

The Supreme Court's decision reversed years of compromise on the issue and set the stage for a final confrontation. Not only did the justices deny Scott's attempt to win his freedom, but they also declared that Congress had no right to limit slavery in the territories at all. Some of the justices said that no black man had the legal right to sue—which meant blacks were not citizens, free or unfree.

Lincoln was shocked. He feared the ruling meant that slavery would soon be legal even in the North. And the idea that blacks were not entitled to the rights of all men cited in the Declaration of Independence offended him deeply. While he probably would have opposed Stephen Douglas for U.S. Senate in 1858 anyway, the race took on even greater meaning.

A HOUSE DIVIDED

Finally the time had come. Abraham Lincoln walked to the front of the Illinois statehouse. The crowd fell silent. Earlier that day, the building had echoed with the raucous shouts of Lincoln's supporters as he was chosen to run for senator on the Republican Party ticket. Now they waited to hear Lincoln's acceptance speech for the nomination—a call to battle for the forces opposed to slavery.

"A house divided against itself cannot stand," Lincoln declared. "I believe this government cannot endure, permanently half *slave* and half *free*. I do not expect the Union to be *dissolved*—I do not expect the house to *fall*—but I *do* expect it will cease to be divided.

"It will become *all* one thing, or *all* the other."

Lincoln's speech, known as the "House Divided" speech, was printed in newspapers across the country. Besides the powerful image of a divided house, which Lincoln took from a story in the Bible, the speech carefully explored the legal issue of slavery and whether a freed man could be enslaved again.

Lincoln warned that the next step would be national slavery. He ended with a blistering attack on Douglas and on the idea that slavery was an issue on which compromise could be reached.

SEVEN DEBATES

Between August and October 1858, Lincoln repeated his basic arguments in countless speeches across the state and in seven debates with Douglas. The Lincoln-Douglas debates are considered a high point of American democracy. They featured two of the country's most important politicians discussing the most important issue facing the nation. They were held in front of real people—often ten thousand or more at a debate—without the interference of commentators or others. Americans across the country followed the debates in newspaper accounts.

"Mr. Lincoln . . . says that this Government cannot endure permanently in the same condition in which it was made by its framers—divided into free and slave states," noted Douglas at the August 21 debate in Ottawa, Illinois. "Why can it not?"

It could, answered the crowd, cheering as Douglas championed states' and voters' rights. "I do not question Mr. Lincoln's conscientious belief that the Negro was made his equal and hence his brother," continued Douglas. Members of the crowd laughed. "But for my own part, I do not regard the Negro as my equal, and positively deny that he is my brother. . . . He belongs to an inferior race, and must always occupy an inferior position."

———————————— ✧ ————————————

Lincoln addresses an Illinois crowd during one of the 1858 debates in the elections. Douglas (left, in black suit) awaits his turn.

Lincoln agreed with the prejudice of the times, but he argued that it did not mean that black people were legally inferior. "I will say here . . . that I have no purpose directly or indirectly to interfere with the institution of slavery in the states where it exists. I, as well as Judge Douglas, am in favor of the race to which I belong having the superior position . . . ," he said, "but I hold that notwithstanding all this, there is no reason in the world why the Negro is not entitled to all the natural rights enumerated in the Declaration of Independence, the rights to life, liberty, and the pursuit of happiness. I hold that he is as much entitled to these as the white man."

The distinction Lincoln made was one often drawn between social classes at the time. Someone of the lower class, as Lincoln had been, might not be the "equal" of someone with a great deal of money or born to a "better" family. But he was entitled to the same rule of law. Saying this of black people was a radical view at the time.

In their debates, Lincoln and Douglas were trying to persuade citizens to elect representatives of their parties to the state government. In turn, these representatives would select the senator. Local concerns and issues besides slavery also played a role in the election. Statewide, the Republicans received more votes. But their victories were concentrated in certain areas. Close races elsewhere prevented them from gaining a majority in the legislature. In the Senate race, Douglas beat Lincoln, fifty-four to forty-six.

Lincoln despaired. He thought his career was over. But within a few days, he told friends, "The fight must go on. The cause of civil liberty must not be surrendered at the end of *one*, or even one *hundred* defeats."

CHAPTER SIX

"RIGHT MAKES MIGHT"

*"No State, upon its own mere motion,
can lawfully get out of the Union."*
—Abraham Lincoln, first inaugural address, 1861

People crowded into the large hall, overflowing into the aisles and out the back of Cooper Union in New York City. Many had come on this cold day, February 27, 1860, out of curiosity—not about what the speaker would say but what he looked like.

They expected a wild man in a funny suit. After all, Abraham Lincoln was a frontiersman born in a tiny cabin far west, more savage than civilized. His speech on this day was part of a lecture series against slavery. Lincoln's address drew so much interest that it had been moved from a church in Brooklyn to the more spacious Cooper Union lecture hall in Manhattan.

Lincoln certainly looked wild when he walked onto the stage. Tall and gawky, he wore clothes that seemed several sizes too small. And his voice! His first words were like squeaks from a warped oboe.

But as the voice steadied, the words took hold of the auditorium. This man was no savage. He was a master at using words to tie together thought and emotion. His speech drilled to the heart of the conflict dividing the country. He addressed Southern slaveholders as if they were in the audience.

"Your purpose then," he thundered, "plainly stated, is that you will destroy the Government, unless you be allowed to construe [explain] and enforce the Constitution as you please, on all points in dispute between you and us."

The crowd roared. Lincoln continued, part lawyer, part rabble-rouser. "But you will not abide [put up with] the election of a Republican president! In that supposed event, you say, you will destroy the Union; and then, you say, the great crime of having destroyed it will be upon us! That is cool. A highwayman holds a pistol to my ear, and mutters through his teeth, 'Stand and deliver, or I shall kill you, and then you will be a murderer!'"

As the crowd cheered him on, Lincoln crafted a careful argument based on the Constitution and the law. He did not call for the abolition of slavery. Although he opposed slavery, he wanted for the moment only to draw a fence around it. But to do that, he challenged the crowd to stand up for its beliefs and do what it considered right.

"Let us have faith that right makes might," he said, "and in that faith, let us, to the end, dare to do our duty as we understand it."

The crowd leapt to its feet with a tremendous roar. The wild man had won their hearts and minds—and maybe their votes for president.

A CANDIDATE?

Lincoln was not officially a candidate for president when he came to New York City that winter, but he was almost surely testing to see what support he had. He had quickly accepted the speaking invitation from a small group of Republicans, even though the trip from Illinois was long and hard.

The trip involved some pleasure as well as business. After Cooper Union, Lincoln went to New England, where his son Robert was attending Phillips Exeter Academy, a private school for boys. But mostly he worked hard. For the next two weeks, he gave speech after speech, bringing the crowds to their feet. The successful speaking tour helped set the stage for Lincoln's candidacy for president in the spring of 1860.

Despite his loss to Douglas, Lincoln was one of the most popular figures in the Republican Party. Other Republican presidential candidates included William H. Seward of New York and Salmon Chase of Ohio, who had helped form the party. But Lincoln had some advantages. He had loyal supporters in Illinois. He was well liked enough to be the second choice of many who supported other candidates. The fact that the Democratic Party nominated Stephen Douglas as their candidate also helped. Many Republicans thought it best for political reasons to nominate their own candidate from the West, and Lincoln was a natural opponent for Douglas.

Lincoln's campaign built momentum at the state nominating convention in Chicago in May. Two Lincoln supporters marched into the gathering with a fence rail that Lincoln was supposed to have split as a boy. The visual image of the rough-hewn wood worked like a modern-day

A campaign poster for Lincoln and his running mate,
Hannibal Hamlin of Maine

———————————————— ✧ ————————————————

public relations campaign. It emphasized Lincoln's rags-to-riches story while reminding people that he was still a common man at heart.

Lincoln won the state nomination easily. Next, his supporters went to work on the national delegates, who were arriving in Chicago for the national Republican convention the following week. The battle settled down to Lincoln and Seward. Lincoln won on the third ballot.

In those days, candidates did not attend their party's convention. They didn't even campaign for president once nominated. Lincoln thought of breaking with this custom, especially after Douglas did so. But in the end, he followed tradition, staying in Springfield while his backers around the country spoke on his behalf.

DIVISIVE ELECTION

The 1860 presidential election was one of the most divided in American history. The explosive issue of slavery split the

Democratic Party in half. The Northern Democrats backed Douglas. But the Southern Democrats nominated John C. Breckinridge of Kentucky—who wanted the federal government to protect slavery. A fourth party, the Constitutional Union Party, nominated John Bell of Tennessee. The party consisted largely of antislavery Whigs and Know-Nothings who had not joined the Republicans.

The four-way split gave Lincoln a big advantage. His party's strength in the North would give him a majority in a widely split race. His campaign also won support by energizing young voters. Calling themselves the Wide Awakes, they dressed in black caps and coats, hoisted split logs on their shoulders, and marched through towns in torch-lit parades. But leaders in the South said they would take their

THE UNDECIDED POLITICAL PRIZE FIGHT.

In this political cartoon, Lincoln and Douglas face off in the boxing ring in the fight for the presidency. The African American helper in Lincoln's corner refers to Lincoln's views on the issue of slavery.

*The Wide Awakes marched through New York City in support
of Lincoln during the 1860 presidential election.*

states out of the Union and form a new nation if Lincoln
were elected.

Before he cast his ballot on election day, Lincoln carefully cut off the presidential portion. He didn't want anyone to think he would selfishly vote for himself.

He didn't have to. Lincoln took a clear majority of the
votes. Right away, several Southern states began taking steps
toward secession, or formal withdrawal from the United States.

GETTING READY

The inauguration would be held in March 1861, so Lincoln's term wouldn't begin for several months. He had
much to do to get ready. He had recently hired a private
secretary, John Nicolay, to help with correspondence and
other matters. Soon he added John Hay to sort and answer
the bundles of mail that arrived every day. Lincoln met
with people in an office at the state capitol almost every
day. The visitors ranged from old friends to job seekers.

After the election, Lincoln began to grow the beard he is famous for. He may have grown it because of a letter from an eleven-year-old girl, Grace Bedell. Lincoln thanked her for the suggestion when he stopped in her hometown of Westfield, New York, en route to Washington. But during the campaign and after the election, many people advised him to grow a beard, since beards were considered distinguished and were becoming fashionable for public figures.

As Lincoln prepared to become president, his wife readied the rest of the family to move east. Robert was attending Harvard and was largely on his own. Thomas, nicknamed "Tad" for Tadpole, was six going on seven. He had a speech defect and was described as overactive and a slow learner, but he was close to his parents and probably was Mary's favorite. Willie had recently turned ten. He was "a smart boy for his age," according to Lincoln's barber.

———————————— ✧ ————————————

Abraham Lincoln (center) *with his secretaries*
John Nicolay (left) *and John Hay* (standing)

Mary took her role as first lady seriously and updated her wardrobe accordingly.

✧ ————————————

Mary went to New York in January to buy formal dresses and other items considered necessary for a first lady. She introduced herself to other women by holding teas and other gatherings. She was worried that her husband would be criticized as vulgar and tried to show that he fit in with proper society.

Lincoln took care of one other piece of personal business before leaving for Washington. He visited his stepmother in Coles County, Illinois, and stopped by his father's grave. Sarah Bush Johnston Lincoln was seventy-three. "Trust in the Lord and all will be well," he told her when it was time to say good-bye. "We will see each other again."

On February 11, 1861, Lincoln stood at the rear of his special train car and waved through the cold rain at a crowd of Springfield well-wishers. "No one, not in my situation, can appreciate my feeling of sadness at this parting," Lincoln told them. "To this place, and the kindness of these people, I owe everything. . . . I now leave, not knowing when, or whether ever, I may return, with a task before me greater than that which rested upon Washington."

The task before Lincoln was to lead a country that was already tearing itself in two. Since the end of December, seven Southern states—South Carolina, Mississippi, Florida, Alabama, Georgia, Louisiana, and Texas—had voted to form a new nation, the Confederate States of America. As tempers flared, troops from South Carolina surrounded Fort Sumter, a federal base, cutting off supplies in an open act of war against the Union. Fort Sumter was a small, only partly finished army post in the harbor outside Charleston, South Carolina. The eighty or so soldiers who huddled behind its walls had come from Fort Moultrie, about a mile closer to the mainland and more vulnerable to attack.

Lincoln's journey to Washington included stops in every major city and most small ones along the way. Massive crowds turned out in Indianapolis, Cincinnati, Columbus, Pittsburgh, Cleveland, Buffalo, Albany, New York City, Philadelphia, Harrisburg, and countless towns along the way. In Buffalo, New York, the mayor dislocated his shoulder in the mad rush to see Lincoln. The president-elect soon lost his voice from giving speeches and thanking people for their support.

For the most part, Lincoln was not critical of the South. "I think that there is no occasion for any excitement," he told the crowd in Cleveland, Ohio. "The crisis, as it is called, is altogether an artificial crisis."

He hadn't lost his sense of humor. "I have come to see you and allow you to see me," he said at a quick stop in Little Falls, New York, "[as far as the ladies are concerned], I have the best of the bargain on my side. I don't make that acknowledgment to the gentlemen."

DEATH PLOT

By the time Lincoln reached Philadelphia, Pennsylvania, the Confederate States of America had chosen a president, Jefferson Davis. U.S. troops in Texas surrendered to the rebel government. And the men in Fort Sumter began running low on supplies.

Threats against Lincoln's life were whispered everywhere. Allan Pinkerton, a famous detective, warned Lincoln of a plot to kill him in Baltimore, Maryland, his next stop after Philadelphia. Pinkerton urged Lincoln to cancel all his speeches and go directly to Washington.

At first Lincoln refused. He went to Independence Hall the next morning as

Confederate president Jefferson Davis

planned. Standing in the place where the United States had been formed, Lincoln promised to preserve the Union.

"I have often inquired of myself what great principle or idea it was that kept this [country] so long together," he said. "It was not the mere matter of the separation of the colonies from the motherland, but something in that Declaration giving liberty, not alone to the people of this country, but hope to the world for all time. . . .

"If this country cannot be saved without giving up that principle . . . I would rather be assassinated on this spot than to surrender it."

But that night, he gave in to the warnings and agreed to sneak into Washington. He did so in disguise, arriving safely. Lincoln was mocked for sneaking into town. But he would face far greater criticism over the next few years.

CHAPTER SEVEN

WAR

"Physically speaking, we cannot separate. We cannot remove our respective sections from each other, nor build an impassable wall between them."
—Abraham Lincoln, first inaugural address, 1861

Sharpshooters stood on the roofs of buildings. Soldiers lined the streets, choking off the intersections. Cannons guarded the approach to the Capitol building. Washington, D.C., had not seen so many armed men ready for battle since the War of 1812.

Lincoln, sitting in an open carriage next to outgoing president James Buchanan, eyed the large crowd warily as they rode from Willard's Hotel to the Capitol on March 4, 1861. When they arrived, Lincoln and the others walked up the steps to the Senate chamber, where Hannibal Hamlin of Maine took the vice president's oath. Then they walked outside for Lincoln's public ceremony. As Lincoln sat, he realized he needed a place for

President Lincoln gives his inaugural address on the steps of the Capitol in Washington, D.C.

his tall hat. Senator Douglas, his longtime foe, kindly took it to hold for him.

Lincoln still hoped for a peaceful settlement to the growing conflict. Several slaveholding states remained in the Union, and some people there were talking of a peaceful solution. Secession could not be permitted. But as Lincoln declared in his inauguration speech, there was still hope.

"My countrymen, one and all, think calmly and *well*, upon this whole subject. Nothing valuable can be lost by taking time," Lincoln told the crowd, describing his own method of making decisions. He addressed Southerners: "In your hands, my dissatisfied countrymen, and not in mine, is the momentous issue of civil war. The government will not assail [attack] you. You can have no conflict without being yourselves the aggressors. You have no oath registered in heaven to destroy the government, while I shall have the most solemn one to 'preserve, protect and defend' it."

The South responded sharply. "It is our wisest policy to accept [the speech] as a declaration of war," wrote an editor in the *Charleston Mercury* newspaper in a typical response.

WAR LOOMS

Surrounded and blocked off, Fort Sumter's small force either had to be resupplied or surrendered. The day after his inauguration, Lincoln asked the commander of the Northern army, General Winfield Scott, how many men it would take to relieve the fort. Scott wanted a force of twenty-five thousand men—nine thousand more than the army possessed.

Lincoln asked the cabinet members (government employees who head important government departments and advise the president) for their opinions. His advisers split. William H. Seward, the secretary of state, argued in favor of surrendering Fort Sumter. He believed that the North should simply wait for some months until tempers cooled. Then the South could be talked into rejoining the Union.

Treasury Secretary Salmon Chase and Postmaster General Montgomery Blair argued that Sumter should be held. Backing down, said Blair, would convince the South that the North wouldn't fight at all.

The split in the cabinet was due to an honest difference of opinions. But personality clashes also existed between various members. Lincoln had not selected men who would blindly go along with his wishes. He wasn't afraid of conflicting opinions. He valued disagreement. But the lack of harmony didn't make things easier.

Militarily, the fort was useless. But surrendering was difficult politically. Lincoln knew that it would make his administration look weak. If he acted too aggressively, however, Virginia and the border states (states that bordered free states and Confederate states) might leave the Union. For three weeks, he did nothing.

When Lincoln finally authorized a relief mission to sail to the fort, delays and confusion slowed it down. The ships were still at sea when, on April 12, Confederate troops began bombing Fort Sumter, forcing it to surrender. The bloodiest war America has ever known had begun.

LIFE AT THE WHITE HOUSE

Slavery was the most important issue dividing the country. But for many of those fighting, from rebel soldiers to Lincoln himself, the real point of the war was states' rights versus the Constitution. Many Southerners believed their states had the right to leave the Union if they wished. Forcing states to stay was the same thing as denying them their rights. But Lincoln saw the Constitution as the supreme law of the land and believed that it did not permit secession. Tear up the Constitution, he thought, and democracy itself would vanish.

After the attack on Fort Sumter, Arkansas, North Carolina, Tennessee, and Virginia joined the seven states that had seceded earlier. Slavery was allowed in four other states: Delaware, Maryland, Kentucky, and Missouri. After Virginia joined the rebellion, several counties in the western part of the state split away (and later formed a new state, West Virginia). Though torn by the conflict, these other slaveholding states did not join the Confederacy. Their support became very important for the Union. Lincoln did nearly anything he could to keep them with the Northern states, which were Maine, New Hampshire, Vermont, New York, Massachusetts, Connecticut, Rhode Island, New

Soldiers with rifles and bayonets stood guard on the White House lawn during the Civil War.

———————————— ✧ ————————————

Jersey, Pennsylvania, Michigan, Ohio, Indiana, Wisconsin, Illinois, Minnesota, Iowa, and Kansas.

Virginia decided to join the Confederacy on April 17. This put rebel forces within an easy march of Washington, D.C. General Scott told Mary Todd Lincoln that she and the boys would be safer outside the city. Mary refused to leave her husband. She downplayed the danger. "Thousands of soldiers are guarding us," she wrote to friends back home, exaggerating quite a bit. "If there is safety in numbers, we have every reason to feel secure. We can only hope for peace."

Mrs. Lincoln threw herself into decorating and repairing the White House, which had been neglected for many years. Unfortunately, she overran her budget within a year of moving in and drew sharp criticism. Like future first ladies, Mary Todd Lincoln became a lightning rod for critics, who found her an easier target than her husband.

Lincoln's sons played games in between the tents of soldiers encamped on the White House grounds. The boys kept goats and a pony, which they occasionally brought

The first family (from left to right): Mary, Willie, Robert, Tad, and Abraham Lincoln

indoors for fun. Tad once rode into the middle of a White House reception on a sled pulled by his goat. Lincoln was an indulgent father and sometimes interrupted work to wrestle with his boys for a few minutes.

The president spent considerably more time wrestling with the problems of the country, however. Lincoln officially started work at 10 A.M., but he almost always started much earlier than that, and he often stayed up past midnight. His secretary John Hay complained that Lincoln failed to keep a regular work schedule, allowing himself to be interrupted by just about anyone. This was an exaggeration, but Lincoln was remarkably accessible. "Anything that kept the people themselves away from him he disapproved," said Hay.

BULL RUN

On Sunday, July 21, 1861, Lincoln worked anxiously in his office, waiting for news from General Scott. After weeks of procrastination, Union forces under the command of

General Irvin McDowell had finally launched an offensive against Confederate troops at Manassas, Virginia. The president and cabinet members had personally reviewed the war plans and approved them. Lincoln had gone to church that morning, praying for the best.

An Office and Home

The White House that Lincoln used as both his home and office sat at the center of a twenty-two-acre property. In addition to the main building, with its exterior very much the same as in modern times, the property included stables, an orchard, outhouses, and farm buildings.

Nearby swamps filled the air with a rotten odor. The rest of the city looked like a small, sleepy town with a few large buildings at the center. The Capitol lacked a dome when Lincoln was inaugurated.

Lincoln used the large room on the south side of the White House as his office, known in modern times as the Lincoln Bedroom. The president and his wife slept in separate, adjoining rooms down the hall. Tad and Willie shared another bedroom. Lincoln's two secretaries, Hay and Nicolay, had their own very small bedrooms at the far end of the hall.

The White House was often filled with job seekers as well as people visiting on official business. After the start of the war, soldiers stayed in the East Room (these days, a large, ceremonial hall) and on the grounds to protect the president's family. But security was much looser than it is in modern times. Lincoln hosted regular open levees, or receptions. Thousands of people squeezed inside the White House twice a week to speak with the president.

A quick and decisive victory might end the rebellion. Throughout the day, the streets were full of rumors of a great victory. Telegrams arrived at the White House late in the afternoon and early evening, confirming the rumors.

At six, Lincoln decided things were going well enough that he could take one of his usual buggy rides through the city. While he was out, Secretary of State Seward rushed into his office.

"Where is the president?" he demanded.

"Gone out," said the secretaries. They showed Seward the telegrams, telling him that the North had won a great victory.

Seward's frown deepened. "Tell no one," he said. "That is not true. The battle is lost."

———————————— ✧ ————————————

Union and Confederate forces clash at the Battle of Bull Run in Manassas, Virginia.

REORGANIZATION

When Lincoln returned, he listened without emotion as John Nicolay told him the news. Through the rest of the night, details of the defeat multiplied. Eyewitnesses rushed into the capital describing the chaos that had followed the Union army's retreat.

The first battle of Manassas, also known as Bull Run, was a serious defeat for the North and a major setback for Lincoln. The Northern army outnumbered the Southern units, but the "Rebs" (the rebels, or Southern army) had the advantages of high ground and fighting on the defensive. While the number of casualties was close—about 625 men died on each side—the battle shattered Union morale. It also ended any illusion that the war would soon be over.

The Union was woefully unprepared to fight. The army had to be expanded by passing special laws, called the draft, requiring men to join the military. Guns and other arms had to be manufactured. Lincoln and his administration set to work. The South faced similar problems, even though it had been preparing for some months. Both sides made many missteps during the first few months of the war as they geared up for battle.

Following the loss at Bull Run, Lincoln appointed General George B. McClellan to reorganize the shattered Army of the Potomac, the force that had been defeated. McClellan proved to be an excellent organizer, rebuilding the army and shaping it into a large fighting force. But he also

General George B. McClellan

proved reluctant to risk that army in battle. At first Lincoln's attitude toward the general and most military leaders could be described as hands-off. He let them make the important decisions about their operations. This was probably because he realized he knew little of military affairs, though he did strive to educate himself by borrowing books from the Library of Congress. Gradually, Lincoln became more assertive and less tolerant when generals didn't achieve the goals he set.

STANTON COMES IN

As the war continued with little progress, Lincoln realized that Secretary of War Simon Cameron wasn't fit for the job. Not only was he unskilled, but rumors were circulating that he was corrupt as well. Still, Lincoln left Cameron in the post until January 1862, when Cameron prepared an official report stating that the government had the right to free slaves and arm them as soldiers. The matter was extremely controversial, especially in the border states.

In December 1861, Lincoln had suggested that Congress consider freeing the slaves—an action known as emancipation. He seems to have been testing the waters or looking for Congress's reaction. But Cameron's statement made it seem like the administration had already decided it could do this on its own, without congressional action.

Lincoln was furious and had the official report rewritten. It

Secretary of War Edwin Stanton

was the last straw—he fired Cameron. In his place, Lincoln appointed Edwin Stanton. It was a stunning choice. Stanton had snubbed Lincoln years before in an important law case. He was also a Democrat, though opposed to slavery. But Lincoln realized that Stanton was a hard worker and would dedicate himself to the Union army.

Meanwhile, Lincoln encouraged his generals, especially McClellan, to battle the enemy. On January 27, 1862, he issued General War Order No. 1: "Ordered that the 22nd day of February 1862, be the day for a general movement of the land and naval forces of the United States against the insurgent [enemy] forces . . . ." McClellan protested Lincoln's plans, suggesting his own instead. Lincoln agreed, as long as he did *something*.

"ACTUALLY GONE"

Shortly after Lincoln issued the war order, his eleven-year-old son Willie got sick. Although doctors at the time didn't know what his illness was, he probably had typhoid fever, which might have been caused by poor sanitation. As Willie's condition worsened, the Lincolns worried. They considered canceling a grand party intended to show off the newly renovated White House. But the doctors assured them that Willie would be fine.

They were wrong. The boy grew worse. He died on February 20, 1862.

"Well, Nicolay, my boy is gone—he is actually gone," Lincoln told his secretary. Tears flooded his eyes as he went on with his work.

Both Lincolns were deeply affected by Willie's death. Mary believed that her husband became much more religious after Willie died. He also drew closer to eight-year-old Tad.

Deeply depressed, Mary stayed in bed for three weeks. When she finally managed to get up, she refused to go into the room where Willie died. She stayed in mourning for a year and often broke down in tears just thinking of her son.

REVERSES

Carrying out his new plans, General McClellan took a large army south in the late winter and early spring of 1862. But he failed to enter battle, saying he needed more men.

"Your [messages] complaining that you are not properly [equipped], while they do not offend me, do pain me very much," Lincoln finally told him in April. "Once more let me

————————————— ◇ —————————————

In this political cartoon, Lincoln is criticized for acting indifferently while thousands of American boys and men fight in the Civil War.

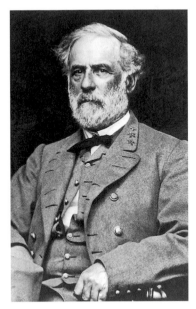

General Robert E. Lee

——— ✧ ———

tell you, it is [necessary] that you strike a blow. . . . I beg to assure you that I have never written you, or spoken to you, in greater kindness of feeling than now. . . . But you must act."

McClellan did act, but his campaign was slow and failed to reach the Confederate capital at Richmond, Virginia. In June 1862, General Robert E. Lee took control of the Confederate army there. His counterattack, remembered in history as the Seven Days' battles, drove the Northern army back on their heels. It added to Lincoln's dissatisfaction with McClellan. Eventually he fired him, reappointed him, then fired him for good.

EMANCIPATION

In early July, Lincoln climbed aboard a carriage to ride to a funeral with Secretary of State Seward and Navy Secretary Gideon Welles. Lincoln's mood was somber. But he had more on his mind than simply grief. He had reached a major decision about the war. "We must free the slaves or be ourselves subdued [conquered]," he told Seward and Welles. He was going beyond his earlier suggestion to Congress to end slavery only in the rebel states.

Seward and Welles, who were both against slavery, reacted cautiously. They feared that outright emancipation would drive the border states into rebellion. But Lincoln insisted

BREAKING THAT "BACKBONE."

This political cartoon, published in 1862, shows Generals Halleck and McClellan using weapons labeled skill and strategy to try to put down the Southern rebellion led by Jefferson Davis (left). Stanton (right) supports a new draft of soldiers, while Lincoln believes that emancipation of the slaves will bring down the Southern states.

————————— ◇ —————————

they think about it. The president felt that the only way to energize the North was to make the moral basis of the war clear, if necessary. And he had decided to take action even without congressional support. As commander in chief of the army and navy, he would declare the slaves free.

In the meantime, Lincoln worked to persuade the public and Congress to move toward his point of view. On July 12, he appealed directly to representatives of the border states to agree to "gradual emancipation." He suggested that blacks could be encouraged to form a new colony in South America. (Historians continue to debate Lincoln's exact feelings on colonization. He had dismissed it as impractical years before, and he took no real action to make it work. Some writers believe that Lincoln only used this argument to make emancipation seem acceptable.)

Congress went ahead and passed a bill stating that anyone rebelling against the government would lose his property. "Property" included slaves, who would be free after sixty days. On July 22, 1862, with the cabinet members gathered around his long office table, the president took out the notes he had been making for weeks and began to read the draft of the Emancipation Proclamation. The heart of the declaration read, "All persons held as slaves within any state, or designated part of a state, the people whereof shall then be in rebellion against the United States shall be

────────────────────── ✧ ──────────────────────

Lincoln meets with General McClellan on the battlefield.

then, thenceforward, and forever free." This meant that all slaves in Southern states would be free.

Although some cabinet members raised objections, Lincoln ended the meeting planning to issue the proclamation. But an argument that Seward made apparently convinced him to hold off. Seward pointed out that the Union armies were not doing well on the battlefield and that the proclamation should be issued after a victory.

FREE AT LAST

In the summer of 1862, Union forces suffered a series of setbacks. General Lee invaded Maryland, and the Northern army fell back. It looked as if Lincoln's victory would never come. Finally, in September, McClellan managed to hold Lee at Antietam, Maryland. Military historians debate whether the Union really won Antietam. Lee withdrew after

——————— ✧ ———————

A Union soldier reads the Emancipation Proclamation to a slave family. The news of freedom brought joy to thousands of black Americans.

A black regiment in the Union Army. After emancipation black soldiers were allowed to join the fight for their freedom.

an indecisive battle, and McClellan failed to follow with a decisive attack. Even Lincoln knew the triumph was less than complete. "The action of the army against the rebels has not been quite what I should have liked," he admitted. But he took it.

On September 22, 1862, Lincoln issued the Emancipation Proclamation freeing slaves in the rebellious states as of January 1, 1863. Slavery could still exist in the states that had not seceded, but its days were numbered.

During and after the Civil War, many blacks honored Lincoln and called him the Great Emancipator. But many other black leaders and white abolitionists at the time believed that Lincoln had not gone far enough. They wanted an end to all slavery everywhere, including the border states.

Black Americans also wanted to fight for their freedom as soldiers. While at first Lincoln had hesitated at this idea, the Emancipation Proclamation allowed black men to join the army. Their role gradually grew from supporting soldiers behind the lines to fighting at the front.

CHAPTER EIGHT

RECONCILIATION

*"I, Abraham Lincoln, President of the United
States, do proclaim, declare, and make known
to all persons who have . . . participated in the
existing rebellion . . . that a full pardon is
hereby granted to each and every one of them."*
—Abraham Lincoln's Proclamation of
Amnesty and Reconstruction, 1863

Lincoln gently urged the horse forward, keeping pace with the
small parade heading toward the battlefield. His mount was tall
and majestic, well matched to his frame. The president towered
over the others in the somber parade. Among the spectators
were soldiers who had been wounded there four months earlier.

More than 150,000 men clashed in and around the town
of Gettysburg, Pennsylvania, during the first few days of July
1863. Twenty-three thousand men from the Northern army
were killed, wounded, or left missing. The casualties on the
Confederate side were higher by five thousand men.

The Union troops won, stopping Lee's march into Pennsylvania. But like many battles in the agonizing war, its significance wasn't obvious at the time. Even in November, as Lincoln rode in the parade to dedicate a cemetery for the dead, Gettysburg seemed to be just one more terrible moment in a war filled with devastation.

Lincoln got off his horse and reviewed some of the escorting troops. He listened with the rest of the crowd as one of the guest speakers, Edward Everett, described the battle in a masterful two-hour speech. And then it was Lincoln's turn. Without his usual nervousness, he began in his best speaking voice:

> *Four score and seven years ago, our fathers brought forth upon this continent a new nation, conceived in Liberty and dedicated to the proposition that all men are created equal.*
>
> *Now we are engaged in a great civil war, testing whether that nation, or any nation, so conceived and so dedicated, can long endure. We are met on a great battlefield of that war. We have come to dedicate a portion of that field, as a final resting place for those who here gave their lives that that nation might live. It is altogether fitting and proper that we should do this.*
>
> *But in a larger sense, we cannot dedicate—we cannot consecrate—we cannot hallow—this ground. The brave men, living and dead, who struggled here, have consecrated it, far above our poor power to add or detract. . . . It is rather for us to be here dedicated to the great task remaining*

Lincoln delivers the Gettysburg Address in November 1863.

———————————— ✧ ————————————

before us . . . that this nation, under God, shall
have a new birth of freedom—and that
government of the people, by the people, for the
people, shall not perish from the earth.

Lincoln's brief speech came to be called the Gettysburg Address. It is considered one of the most eloquent statements of American political beliefs ever made.

TURNING POINT

Much later, 1863 would be viewed as an important year in the Civil War. Union armies won a key victory at Vicksburg, Mississippi, as well as at Gettysburg. Despite riots and protests against the draft, Lincoln insisted that it must continue. He also supported unpopular taxes and suspended habeas corpus, an important legal right for those accused of a crime.

Though his party did poorly in the elections for Congress, by the end of 1863 Lincoln's popularity had begun to rise. Many citizens praised the Emancipation Proclamation. And his efforts to build the army, which included personally testing weapons, had begun to pay off on the battlefield. He was finally finding competent generals.

None was more important than the victor of Vicksburg, Ulysses S. Grant. In February 1864, Lincoln promoted Grant to the newly created rank of lieutenant general. The next month, he put him in charge of the entire army.

SEANCES

Mary Lincoln had suffered greatly since the death of her son Willie. At some point during her mourning, she began hosting gatherings called seances. A clairvoyant (someone who claims to perceive things that are unseen or not heard by others) claimed to contact the boy in the afterlife. Mary said she was also visited by the Lincolns' other dead son and various Union officers offering advice on the war.

"Willie lives," Mary told her half-sister. "He comes to me every night and stands at the foot of the bed with the same sweet smile he always has had. He does not always come alone. Little Eddie is sometimes with him."

Lincoln did not share his wife's beliefs, but he tolerated her as he always had and did not interfere with the seances. After Willie's death, he had drawn even closer to Tad. The boy often played in his father's office when Lincoln worked late. Lincoln packed him off to his own bed when he fell asleep.

As close as Lincoln was to Tad, he remained distant from his oldest son, Robert. Their cool relationship was similar to

Thomas "Tad" Lincoln dressed in a Union soldier's uniform
✧ ——————————————

the one Lincoln had had with his own father. Robert wanted to join the army during the war. Lincoln, probably because of Mary's objections, refused to let him. Finally he asked Grant to take Robert on his staff. Robert joined at the very end of the war as a captain, though his duties were light.

REELECTION

As Lincoln prepared for the presidential election of 1864, he faced a number of opponents for the Republican Party nomination. Among the most important was his own treasury secretary, Salmon Chase.

It seems surprising, but many party leaders were dissatisfied with Lincoln. Some abolitionists worried he would end the war without completely abolishing slavery. Other Northerners were convinced that Lincoln favored the South. Still other politicians wanted power for themselves. Some simply felt they could do a better job.

Chase was one of these. But the president seems to have had little trouble outmaneuvering him and others.

He shrewdly sprang into action early in 1864, long before the election. On January 7, Lincoln's friends helped persuade Republicans in New Hampshire to pass a resolution backing Lincoln. It was a jolt for Chase, because he had been born in New Hampshire and expected support there. Two days later, the Pennsylvania legislature also backed Lincoln.

Chase's supporters struck back with an anonymous statement attacking Lincoln. But the statement hurt Chase and helped Lincoln by creating sympathy for the president. Embarrassed, Chase offered to resign his job.

"Whether you shall remain at the head of the Treasury Department is a question which I will not allow myself to consider from any standpoint other than my judgment of [your] public service," said Lincoln, after mentioning that he had not read the pamphlet attacking him. "And in that view, I do not perceive occasion for a change."

Recognizing that he was beaten, Chase withdrew from the presidential race. Lincoln

————————————✧

Treasury Secretary Salmon Chase failed to stop Lincoln's bid for reelection.

won easy victories in the state conventions, assuring his place on the ticket. The Democrats nominated General George B. McClellan. McClellan, whom Lincoln had fired before Gettysburg, campaigned for an immediate end to the war.

Northern victories that summer and fall helped boost Lincoln's standing. Grant proved relentless as he marshaled his forces and threw them directly against Lee. Under Grant's direction, General William Tecumseh Sherman marched into Atlanta, Georgia, on September 2. His victory there set the stage for a devastating campaign of destruction by Northern armies as they pressed southward. In the election in November, Lincoln won 55 percent of the vote, defeating McClellan in a landslide victory.

NEW PROBLEMS AND GOALS

Well before the election was held, Lincoln had begun thinking about his next term and the end of the war. Three important questions had to be answered:

1) What should be done about slavery, which still existed in the border states?
2) Could black people be full citizens if they weren't slaves?
3) What should be done with the South when the war was over?

Lincoln's answer to the first question was that slavery must be abolished forever—but only by legal means. After his reelection, he pushed Congress for action, contacting Democrats as well as Republicans. On January 31, 1865, legislators passed the Thirteenth Amendment. It declared, "Neither slavery nor involuntary servitude, except as a punishment for crime whereof the party shall

Members of the U.S. House of Representatives reacted with a range of feelings after the Thirteenth Amendment—banning slavery— was passed on January 31, 1865.

have been duly convicted, shall exist within the United States, or any place subject to their jurisdiction. Congress shall have power to enforce this article by appropriate legislation." At long last, slavery could no longer exist in the United States.

RECONSTRUCTION

But the questions about the future of the South and the rights of blacks were not so easily answered. The Republican Party was divided about how harshly to treat Southern states when they were "reconstructed," or rebuilt and brought back into the Union after the war. These issues dominated American politics for the next several years.

Lincoln had already offered pardons to Southerners who were willing to pledge their allegiance to the United States.

Lincoln's public statements hedged on the issue of voting rights for blacks. But he told a fellow Republican in 1864 that he was in favor of "at least, suffrage [voting rights] on the basis of intelligence and military service" for blacks.

Early in the war, Louisiana had been retaken by the North. Lincoln's reconstruction policies there emphasized self-government—leaders were chosen by the people, not appointed by Lincoln or the army. Blacks were required to hold jobs or take government-paid work. Army personnel supervised private companies where blacks worked to prevent the employees from abuses such as whippings.

"It was a step up from slavery," wrote historian Phillip Shaw Paludan, "but it drew the fire of reformers who wanted freedom for black workers to mean the same thing as it meant for whites." Full equality meant equal pay and the right to work (or not work) under humane conditions.

Lincoln aimed to gradually rebuild the devastated South and preserve democracy. He headed off harsh reconstruction plans proposed by various Northern congressmen. As 1865 began and the end of the war seemed near, the president aimed to make his second inaugural speech a message of reconciliation and renewal for the country.

RECONCILIATION

On a wet, windy March 4, 1865, Lincoln waded through the muddy streets and entered the Capitol to be sworn in a second time. As he stepped outside to deliver his speech, the sun burst through the clouds.

"On the occasion corresponding to this four years ago," he began, unfurling the large sheet his speech was printed on, "all thoughts were anxiously directed to an impending civil war. . . .

"Neither party expected for the war the magnitude, or the duration, which it has already attained. Neither anticipated that the cause of the conflict might cease with, or even before, the conflict itself should cease. . . . Both read the same Bible, and pray to the same God; and each invokes His aid against the other."

Lincoln then suggested that God gave America—both North and South—the war as punishment for the terrible sin of slavery. The whole country, he suggested, shared in the guilt.

He concluded, "With malice toward none, with charity for all . . . let us strive . . . to bind up the nation's wounds, to . . . achieve and cherish a just, and a lasting peace. . . . "

───────────── ✧ ─────────────

In Lincoln's second inaugural address, he spoke about rebuilding the nation after the devastating effects of the divisive Civil War.

MANY ACHIEVEMENTS

Lincoln is remembered mainly for his involvement with the Civil War, but his administration had other accomplishments. One important achievement was to encourage the development of the cross-country, transcontinental railroad. In the years following Lincoln's death, the railroad opened up the West to more settlement while strengthening business and communication among the states.

Lincoln also signed the Homestead Act of 1862, which allowed any citizen living on public land for five years to become its owner. This law also spurred western settlement. The Morrill Act, named after Vermont congressman Justin S. Morrill and supported by Lincoln, established agricultural and engineering colleges in every state.

In 1869 the tracks of the Union Pacific and the Central Pacific Railroads met in Utah, completing the first transcontinental railroad in the United States.

Confederate general Lee (right) *surrenders to Union general Grant* (left)
at Appomattox Court House, Virginia, officially ending the Civil War.

VICTORY AT LAST

After the inauguration, General Grant and his troops continued their pursuit of the last major Confederate armies,
which were under the command of General Lee in central
Virginia. Finally, on April 9, 1865, Lee surrendered at
Appomattox Court House, Virginia. When the news reached
Lincoln, he was overjoyed. The war was over. On April 11,
he gave a speech urging reconciliation with the South. He
declared that blacks who were educated and those who had
served in the army should be allowed to vote.

"This means [black] citizenship," said a man in the
crowd, echoing the angry and prejudiced views of many
others. "That is the last speech he will ever make."

The man was John Wilkes Booth.

Ford's Theatre
———— ◇ ————

GOOD FRIDAY

April 14, 1865, was Good Friday, the Friday before Easter. It was not a holiday for Lincoln or his cabinet members. Although the war was nearly over, the job of healing the nation's wounds would be just as difficult. Lincoln worked well into the evening, then finally stopped to get ready for the night's entertainment. He and his wife were going to Ford's Theatre, where a play called *Our American Cousin* was being performed.

Abe and Mary Lincoln showed up at the theater a little after nine. They were accompanied by an army major, Henry Reed Rathbone, and his fiancée, Clara Harris. Meanwhile, Lincoln's bodyguard, John F. Parker, stationed himself in the hallway outside the president's box.

Although the show was in progress when the Lincolns entered, the thousand or so spectators stood and cheered as the president took his seat. Lincoln waved, then sat back in his chair, out of view. At some point after the president arrived, Parker left his post outside the box and went to find a drink.

John Wilkes Booth had been waiting all day for just such a chance. He knew the theater well. He was one of the

country's most famous actors. He was also a strong supporter of the South and a fanatical racist. The only way to
prevent blacks from taking over, he believed, was to kill
Abraham Lincoln.

Earlier in the day, Booth had altered the door mecha-
nism to be able to get into Lincoln's box. Now the path
was clear. He opened the door and entered quietly.

Booth stepped up, straightened his arm, then fired a small
pistol point-blank into the back of Lincoln's head. The bullet
crashed through his brain and stopped near his right eye.

————————————— ✧ —————————————

*John Wilkes Booth shoots President Lincoln
at Ford's Theatre on April 14, 1865.*

Lincoln's assassin, John Wilkes Booth

———————— ✧ ————————

Rathbone jumped up and struggled with Booth. The assassin slashed Rathbone's arm with a dagger, then leapt to the stage ten feet below. As he landed, the spur on his heel caught in an American flag. He stumbled and broke his shin.

"*Sic semper tyrannis,*" Booth shouted. The Latin phrase means, "So it is with tyrants."

"He has shot the President!" yelled someone in the theater. And then everything was chaos.

EPILOGUE

LEGACY

At long last, the somber procession reached the end of its journey. The ornate coffin was lifted from the railroad car and escorted to the state capitol building. It had taken several weeks for the coffin to come home to Springfield. Massive crowds had gathered across the nation to mourn Lincoln. Finally it was Springfield's turn to put him to rest. Seventy-five thousand mourners paid their respects in the statehouse. Then, on May 4, 1865, Lincoln was buried in the Oak Ridge Cemetery near Springfield.

During the Civil War, more than 620,000 Union and Confederate soldiers were killed. Abraham Lincoln was one of the war's last victims. His assassin, Booth, died from wounds he received before surrendering on April 26. Four others were hanged for their involvement in Booth's conspiracy, which was intended to include the assassinations of Vice President Andrew Johnson and Secretary of State William Seward. (Seward was stabbed but recovered. Johnson was not harmed.)

Thousands of mourners paid their last respects as Lincoln's body made its final journey home to Springfield, Illinois.

Mary Todd Lincoln's mental state deteriorated sharply after her husband's death. She was committed to an insane asylum by her son Robert for a short time but was soon released. She died in 1882. Tad died in 1871 at the age of eighteen. Robert had a successful career as a lawyer, diplomat, and businessman. He died in 1926.

Lincoln's achievement in holding the United States together during the Civil War is considered one of the most important accomplishments in American history. Lincoln is known above all as the president who freed the slaves, the man who held the country together in its darkest hour, and the statesman who laid the groundwork for a rebirth of American democracy.

But he is more. In many ways, Lincoln represents the American dream of democracy and equality. "He was not a born king of men," said newspaper editor and abolitionist Horace Greeley, "but a child of the people."

Poor but willing to work hard, Lincoln taught himself a range of subjects, including the law. An honest man, he paid large personal debts that others might have run from. Disappointed and defeated in politics, he kept fighting until he finally won. Suffering great personal losses, he comforted others. Wracked by depression, he managed to remain hopeful for his country's future. He learned from his mistakes and held firmly to his beliefs. For all of these reasons, Americans consider him the country's greatest president of the past—and a model for the future.

———————————————— ✧ ————————————————

Lincoln saw the United States through the most divisive time in its history. Supporters and critics of his policies would all agree that he was an honest and fair man.

TIMELINE

1809   Abraham Lincoln is born to Thomas and Nancy Hanks Lincoln in Hodgenville, Kentucky.

1815   Lincoln briefly attends school with his older sister, Sarah. He attends school on and off over the years, never for very long.

1818   Lincoln's mother dies of "milk sickness."

1819   Lincoln's father marries Sarah Bush Johnston, who brings her own three children into the family.

1830   The Lincoln family moves to Macon County, Illinois.

1831   Hired by an area businessman, Lincoln, his stepbrother John Johnston, and his cousin John Hanks build a flatboat and travel to New Orleans. When they return, Lincoln takes a job in New Salem, where he works as a store clerk.

1832   Lincoln runs for the Illinois legislature and loses. He serves in the militia during the Black Hawk War.

1834   Lincoln wins election to the Illinois House of Representatives.

1835   Lincoln's friend and possible fiancée, Ann Rutledge, dies in August, leaving him deeply depressed.

1836   After years of studying on his own, Lincoln receives his license to practice law. The following year, he moves to Springfield and takes a job as the law partner of John T. Stuart.

1842   Lincoln marries Mary Todd.

1844   Lincoln forms a law partnership with William H. Herndon.

1846   Lincoln is elected to the U.S. Congress, serving only one term because of an agreement to rotate the seat among several Whig candidates.

1850 The Lincolns' son Edward dies on February 1. Lincoln returns home to Springfield, where he devotes himself to his law practice and family.

1854 The U.S. Congress votes to allow slavery in the territories. Lincoln sees this as a dangerous step.

1855 Lincoln loses his bid to represent Illinois in the U.S. Senate.

1856 With the Whig Party breaking up, Lincoln joins the new Republican Party.

1858 Lincoln participates in seven debates with Democrat Stephen Douglas. Lincoln loses his bid to unseat Douglas as U.S. senator.

1860 Lincoln is elected president of the United States. Several Southern states threaten to leave the Union.

1861 The Civil War starts in April when the Confederates fire on Fort Sumter in South Carolina. Shocked by defeat at Bull Run, the North prepares for a long war.

1862 The Lincolns' son Willie dies, probably of typhoid fever. Following the Union victory at Antietam, Maryland, Lincoln issues the Emancipation Proclamation, freeing all slaves in the South.

1863 Lincoln delivers the Gettysburg Address, considered one of the finest speeches ever given.

1864 Lincoln wins reelection in the fall and begins planning for the end of the war.

1865 Lincoln engineers the passage of the Thirteenth Amendment, abolishing slavery in America. The Civil War ends on April 9, when Confederate general Robert E. Lee surrenders to Union general Ulysses S. Grant. Five days later, Lincoln is assassinated by John Wilkes Booth at Ford's Theatre in Washington, D.C.

SOURCE NOTES

8 Carl Sandburg, *Abraham Lincoln: The Prairie Years*, vol. 1 (New York: Harcourt, Brace & Co., 1926), 136–137.

9 Abraham Lincoln, *Speeches and Writings 1859–1865*, ed. Don E. Fehrenbacker (New York: The Library of America, 1989), 162.

10 Sandburg, *Abraham Lincoln: The Prairie Years*, vol. 1, 21.

11 Lincoln, *Speeches and Writings 1859–1865*, 162.

11 David Herbert Donald, *Lincoln* (New York: Simon & Schuster, 1995), 23.

14 Ibid., 26.

14 Ibid., 42.

15 Ibid., 43.

15 Ibid., 30.

16 William H. Herndon and Jesse W. Weik, *Herndon's Life of Lincoln*, eds. Paul M. Angle and Henry Steele Commager (New York: DaCapo Press, 1983), 37.

19 Lincoln, *Speeches and Writings 1859–1865*, 164.

19–20 Herndon and Weik, *Herndon's Life of Lincoln*, 67–68.

21 Kenneth J. Winkle, *The Young Eagle* (Dallas: Taylor Trade Publishing, 2001), 63.

21 Abraham Lincoln, *Speeches and Writings 1832–1858*, ed. Don E. Fehrenbacker (New York: The Library of America, 1989), 1.

22 Ibid., 4.

22 Ibid., 5.

23 Donald, *Lincoln*, 45.

25 Winkle, *The Young Eagle*, 116.

26 Herndon and Weik, *Herndon's Life of Lincoln*, 113.

27 Lincoln, *Speeches and Writings 1832–1858*, 69.

27–28 Herndon and Weik, *Herndon's Life of Lincoln*, 148–49.

31 Donald, *Lincoln*, 85.

35 Lincoln, *Speeches and Writings 1859–1865*, 245.

35–36 Donald, *Lincoln*, 97.

39 Lincoln, *Speeches and Writings 1832–1858*, 138.

39 Lincoln, *Speeches and Writings 1859–1865*, 363.

40 Lincoln, *Speeches and Writings 1832–1858*, 139.

40 Ibid.

40 Ibid., 140.

44 Donald, *Lincoln*, 137.

44 Herndon and Weik, *Herndon's Life of Lincoln*, 246–247.

47 Lincoln, *Speeches and Writings 1832–1858*, 316.

49 Ibid.

50 Herndon and Weik, *Herndon's Life of Lincoln*, 301.

50 Lincoln, *Speeches and Writings 1832–1858*, 356.

51 Ibid., 303.

52 Herndon and Weik, *Herndon's Life of Lincoln*, 312.

52 Ibid., 313.

54 Lincoln, *Speeches and Writings 1832–1858*, 426.

55 Ibid., 505.

55 Ibid., 512.

56 Ibid.

56 Ibid., 831.

57 Lincoln, *Speeches and Writings 1859–1865*, 218.

58 Ibid., 126.

58 Ibid., 127.

58 Ibid., 130.

63 Jean H. Baker, *Mary Todd Lincoln: A Biography* (New York: W. W. Norton, 1987), 210.

64 Donald, *Lincoln*, 271.

64 Ibid., 273.

65 Lincoln, *Speeches and Writings 1859–1865*, 206.

65 Ibid., 208.
66 Ibid., 213.
67 Ibid., 221.
68 Ibid., 223–224.
69 Carl Sandburg, *Abraham Lincoln: The War Years*, vol. 1 (New York: Harcourt, Brace & Co., 1939), 137.
71 Baker, *Mary Todd Lincoln: A Biography*, 184.
72 Herndon and Weik, *Herndon's Life of Lincoln*, 415.
74 Sandburg, *Abraham Lincoln: The War Years*, vol. 1, 302.
77 Lincoln, *Speeches and Writings 1859–1865*, 303.
77 Donald, *Lincoln*, 336.
79 Lincoln, *Speeches and Writings 1859–1865*, 313–314.
79 Donald, *Lincoln*, 362.
80 Lincoln, *Speeches and Writings 1859–1865*, 341.
81–82 Ibid., 368.
83 James M. McPherson, *Battle Cry of Freedom* (New York: Oxford University Press, 1988), 557.
84 Lincoln, *Speeches and Writings 1859–1865*, 555.
85–86 Ibid., 536.
87 Baker, *Mary Todd Lincoln: A Biography*, 220.
89 Lincoln, *Speeches and Writings 1859–1865*, 577.
92 McPherson, *Battle Cry of Freedom*, 702.
92 Phillip Shaw Paludan, *The Presidency of Abraham Lincoln* (Lawrence, KS: University Press of Kansas, 1994), 245–246.
92–93 Lincoln, *Speeches and Writings 1859–1865*, 686.
93 Ibid., 687.
95 McPherson, *Battle Cry of Freedom*, 852.
98 Carl Sandburg, *Abraham Lincoln: The War Years*, vol. 4 (New York: Harcourt, Brace & Co., 1939), 282.
98 Ibid.
100 William A. DeGregorio, *The Complete Book of U.S. Presidents* (New York: Wings Books, 1991), 242.

SELECTED BIBLIOGRAPHY

Baker, Jean H. *Mary Todd Lincoln: A Biography.* New York: W. W. Norton, 1987.

Chisholm, Daniel. *The Civil War Notebook of Daniel Chisholm.* Edited by W. Springer Menge and J. August Shimrak. New York: Orion Books, 1989.

Davis, William C., ed. *Diary of a Confederate Soldier: John S. Jackman of the Orphan Brigade.* Columbia, SC: University of South Carolina Press, 1990.

Donald, David Herbert. *Lincoln.* New York: Simon & Schuster, 1995.

Fletcher, William A. *Rebel Private: Front and Rear.* New York: Dutton, 1995.

Grant, Ulysses S. *Memoirs and Selected Letters.* Edited by Mary Drake McFeely and William S. McFeely. New York: The Library of America, 1990.

Herndon, William H., and Jesse W. Weik. Edited by Paul M. Angle and Henry Steele Commager. *Herndon's Life of Lincoln.* New York: DaCapo Press, 1983.

Johnson, Paul. *A History of the American People.* New York: Harper Collins, 1997.

Kunhardt, Philip B. Jr., Philip B. Kunhardt III, and Peter W. Kunhardt. *Lincoln.* New York: Alfred A. Knopf, 1992.

Lincoln, Abraham. *Speeches and Writings 1832–1858.* Edited by Don E. Fehrenbacker. New York: The Library of America, 1989.

_____. *Speeches and Writings 1859–1865.* Edited by Don E. Fehrenbacker. New York: The Library of America, 1989.

McPherson, James M. *Battle Cry of Freedom.* New York: Oxford University Press, 1988.

Morison, Samuel Eliot, and Henry Steele Commager. *The Growth of the American Republic.* Vol. 1. New York: Oxford University Press, 1950.

Nicolay, John G., and John Hay. *Abraham Lincoln: A History.* Edited by Paul M. Angle. Chicago: The University of Chicago Press, 1966.

Paludan, Phillip Shaw. *The Presidency of Abraham Lincoln*. Lawrence, KS: University Press of Kansas, 1994.

Sandburg, Carl. *Abraham Lincoln: The Prairie Years*. Vols. 1 & 2. New York: Harcourt, Brace & Co., 1926.

_____. *Abraham Lincoln: The War Years*. Vols. 1–4. New York: Harcourt, Brace & Co., 1939.

Singletary, Otis A. *The Mexican War*. Chicago: The University of Chicago Press, 1960.

Tarbell, Ida, and J. McCan Davis. *The Early Life of Abraham Lincoln*. New York: S. S. McClure Limited, 1896.

Wills, Garry. *Lincoln at Gettysburg: The Words That Remade America*. New York: Simon & Schuster, 1992.

Winkle, Kenneth J. *The Young Eagle*. Dallas: Taylor Trade Publishing, 2001.

FURTHER READING AND WEBSITES

There are thousands of books, websites, films, and videos devoted to Abraham Lincoln and his times. Here are just a few.

On Lincoln:

"Abraham Lincoln Papers at the Library of Congress." *American Memory Library of Congress*. March 1, 2002. <http://memory.loc .gov/ammem/alhtml/malhome.html> (March 27, 2003). This site introduces the Library of Congress collection of Lincoln's letters.

Bial, Raymond. *Where Lincoln Walked*. New York: Walker & Co., 1997.

Freedman, Russell. *Lincoln: A Photobiography*. New York: Clarion Books, 1987.

"The History Place Presents Abraham Lincoln." *The History Place.* 1996–2003. <http://www.historyplace.com/lincoln> (March 27, 2003). This is an illustrated timeline of Lincoln's life with links to other articles and documents.

Holzer, Harold, ed. *Abraham Lincoln, the Writer.* Honesdale, PA: Boyds Mills Press, 2000.

"Lincoln Home National Historic Site." *National Park Service.* November 12, 2002. <http://www.nps.gov/liho> (March 27, 2003). This is the National Park Service site about Lincoln's Springfield home.

"Lincoln/Net." *Northern Illinois University.* 2000. <http://lincoln.lib .niu.edu> (March 27, 2003). This site contains a wide range of primary materials on Lincoln's Illinois years.

Schott, Jane A. *Abraham Lincoln.* Minneapolis: Lerner Publications Company, 2002.

Sullivan, George. *Abraham Lincoln.* New York: Scholastic Reference, 2000.

On the Civil War:

Arnold, James, and Roberta Wiener. *Divided in Two: The Road to Civil War, 1861.* Minneapolis: Lerner Publications Company, 2002.

_____. *Life Goes On: The Civil War at Home, 1861–1865.* Minneapolis: Lerner Publications Company, 2002.

Catton, Bruce. *The American Heritage Picture History of the Civil War.* New York: American Heritage Publishing, 1960.

Damon, Duane. *Growing Up in the Civil War 1861 to 1865.* Minneapolis: Lerner Publications Company, 2003.

_____. *When This Cruel War Is Over: The Civil War Home Front.* Minneapolis: Lerner Publications Company, 1996.

Davis, William C., Brian C. Pohanka, and Don Troiani, eds. *Civil War Journal: The Leaders.* Nashville, TN: Rutledge Hill Press, 1997.

Day, Nancy. *Your Travel Guide to Civil War America.* Minneapolis: Lerner Publications Company, 2001.

Murphy, Jim. *The Long Road to Gettysburg.* New York: Clarion Books, 1992.

On Slavery and Emancipation:

Burchard, Peter. *Lincoln and Slavery.* New York: Atheneum, 1999.

The Civil War. Directed by Ken Burns. Florentine Films/WETA-Washington/Pacific Arts Video, 1990. Videocassette.

Greene, Meg. *Slave Young, Slave Long: The American Slave Experience.* Minneapolis: Lerner Publications Company, 1999.

Heinrichs, Ann. *The Emancipation Proclamation.* Minneapolis: Compass Point Books, 2002.

INDEX

ABOUT THE AUTHOR

Jeremy Roberts is the author of many books for young readers, including biographies of Joan of Arc, George Washington, and Tiger Woods.

❖

PHOTO ACKNOWLEDGMENTS